He Who Shouts Loudest

by
Ed Davey

authorHOUSE®

AuthorHouse™ UK Ltd.
500 Avebury Boulevard
Central Milton Keynes, MK9 2BE
www.authorhouse.co.uk
Phone: 08001974150

First published by AuthorHouse 11/1/2007

ISBN: 978-1-4343-2906-6 (sc)

Printed in the United States of America
Bloomington, Indiana

This book is printed on acid-free paper.

Contents

Foreword.

2007 started well, really well, but then very quickly spiralled out of control. New Years Eve had been full of resolutions, big ones; one's that mattered! It felt like a platform for a whole new beginning. Life can be like that. One minute everything seems full of opportunity and heading in the right direction and then suddenly the wheels can fall off in quick succession. Relationships, family, work and health are the significant issues in most people's lives. For various reasons my first three had already suffered during 2006. My 14 year marriage had fizzled out and after a 20 year commitment to the family business my continuing involvement within it was in doubt too which was doing nothing for either family relations or progressing my career. All I really had going for me was my health. Nonetheless I had a clear vision of how to resolve the challenges facing me.

As a result of my recent various life changing experiences, I had recently applied some very positive thinking towards meeting all of my challenges at 42 years of age. In an era when Jonny Wilkinson's 27 points tally at Twickenham against the Scots was being venerated as one of the greatest sporting comebacks in the history of rugby there were at least a few inspirational role models to look towards. If he could shake off years of frustrating injury to make a comeback of such staggering brilliance I was sure I could achieve my goals.

However, I wouldn't be drawing a lot of inspiration from our country's leaders, as on the political scene there was an abundant amount of ineptitude being demonstrated by all and sundry. The majority of the cabinet had been questioned, invited to police stations or even been arrested as the Cash for Honours' Enquiry rumbled on. Margaret Beckett should have been in Iran and Des Browne ought to have been sewing up flak jackets for Iraq. John Reid should have been filling the cement mixer for the foundations of Lord Levy's cell just in case they found him guilty and Patricia Hewitt was expected to have been sorting out the NHS crisis. Unfortunately they were all too busy getting their stories straight for their interviews with the Metropolitan Police. Interestingly during this time Tony Blair reported to the Liaison Committee and sounded chronically vague on the major health issues facing the UK. He seemed strangely upbeat and positive about the NHS and its achievements. In the regions, however, the NHS seemed to be in reverse to the Prime ministers claims. New figures revealed that "bed blocking" in Lincolnshire hospitals had nearly doubled in a year. There had been an 80% rise in the number of patients blocking beds. From 76 in mates taking up 630 bed days in 2005, the situation had deteriorated to 90 POW's taking up 1,138 bed days exactly a year later. In the very hospital I found myself in, the Primary Care Trust was pushing for Ward closures for the elderly with a view to pushing their care out to hospices whilst the nursing staff fought to keep the ward opened on the grounds of a growing need for the facility. A month or two later, just up the road from Lincolnshire in the East Riding, people were so concerned about what was happening in their hospitals that they started protesting. Through marching and shouting they attempted to demonstrate their lack of confidence in their local PCT's. There appeared to be a dichotomy between the government's perception in the big smoke and the reality on the ground in the leafy lanes of the countryside and the regions.

I was to fall into the hands of the enemy unknowingly on a lonely cold January evening when I became unexpectedly ill. Despite various attempts to escape I was subjected to a realistic day to day insight into our local health service which unexpectedly frightened me nearly to death. I experienced the national health service of an alleged industrialized modern democracy which I walked into with a completely blank mind and other than the usual super bug concerns and what one picks out of the daily rags, not too many opinions. By the time I left I had experienced moments when I expected the Monty Python team to leap from behind a screen wearing their full doctors and nurses outfits with John Cleese as the lead declaring "It's a Joke – sorry, Health Service- none of these people are really ill – we've just dressed 'em up to look ill – Honest ! Just look at this one, thinks he's dying, got years in him yet, haven't you mate? Mate? You awake? Gawd he's only bloody copped it! Can you believe it? People today!"

I have always been fortunate enough through my work to afford private health care. Whenever I had needed the help and support of the health service in the past it had always been through the private system. I had received various standards of care within the private sector. I was well aware that it was not a panacea and as I entered the NHS I was not expecting a great deal of difference from my experiences of the health service so far. I had never made a conscious decision to not use the NHS. It was just that I didn't need to. Because of this I walked into its environment as a slightly naïve, hopeful case expecting the sort of care associated with the 21st Century. I never expected to be a critic and I am no expert. It was never in my mind to spend hours upon my recovery writing about my experiences. Certainly my experience is very individual and reflects a small cross section of the NHS. There are plenty of hospitals and departments which I am sure I would greatly appreciate and many people who work in the health service who will find this story difficult to digest at times. Nevertheless there are many diverse issues within our enormous health service, some of which I did have the misfortune to experience and despite how we are often treated as patients, despite how autocratic and conceited the consultants might be and despite how the politicians control and tinker with it, it is still 'our health service' and we should be interested enough in it, to want it to improve.

Tony Blair, Patricia Hewitt and the Caroline Flints of this world have a lot to answer for, because in my mind they made a flawed assumption and forgot this very concept. One eminent local surgeon recently described the health service to me as being full of personnel with various substandard degrees of intelligence; "It's got nitwits, halfwits and even 'Hewitts' in it".

Politicians believe they are in control; having seen what I have seen, I am convinced otherwise. But they are not alone in sharing the responsibility for the debacle of the NHS. A recent report in the news that over a quarter of NHS trusts are culpable of financial mismanagement tends to indicate that the incompetence is beyond just the politician's control. I'm sure that when health policies and budgets are put in place by the cabinet and health departments the politicians naively assume the resources will be managed to their optimum. Unfortunately the management of trusts like any business is dependent upon the ability and the vision of those in charge. Like all successful organisations, the quality of the leadership is a fundamental requirement to the organisations performance despite the size of the resource deployed towards its success. Even so in an era when government policy is advocating massive investment in data base technology in order to improve their delivery of service, we are also subjected to government departmental incompetence on a massive scale. It is extremely concerning for all of us to hear the recent debacle surrounding the works and pensions department's mailing of confidential financial information to all of the wrong pensioners. Imagine crossing over to the health service with the same level of ineptitude; how would you like the NHS to send someone else all of your medical details? Yet the problems are not even that simply explained as in addition we are subjected to stories that 70% of the NHS trusts in the UK are under severe financial pressure as a result of government targets. An ageing population as a result of low birth rates and longer lives and an ever increasing demand upon services due to liberal immigration policies are contributing towards the problem. You don't have to be a rocket scientist to figure out that a crisis is on the horizon when resources are being limited by new government budget cut backs at a time when demand upon services are peaking. Upon the retirement of Tony Blair and with his understudy Gordon Brown coming to the fore, one can predict that the management of the NHS will become a political pawn of hefty significance with many promises made about how much more effort will go towards achieving success in place of the numerous failures of the past. Let's face it there have been 9 major re-organisations of the NHS in the last 10 years with the most recent resulting in another crisis as the NHS found itself critically short of junior doctors. We are about to see Gordon Brown and David Cameron waste their breath as they argue a point of difference about giving hospitals and GPs more autonomy and more scope so that private and voluntary sector providers can supply their services to the NHS. They will pontificate across the commons floor strutting like proud peacocks whilst they try to emulate great speakers of the past. It makes one wonder how much effort actually goes into presentation compared to serious policy reform. Either way it all seems such a waste of time as it's like putting a sticking plaster over a gaping wound. They are usually just clipping around the edges rather than mowing the lawn. It would be much more appropriate to apply major surgery whilst the patient was still alive and sort out the NHS once and for all rather than lending it minor assistance and never healing the beast.

As I said I'm not a health care expert, but in all of my experiences throughout my relatively short stay I learnt that it was not beneficial to be totally reliant upon the NHS. I became very concerned for the millions of people who are entirely dependent upon it for their care and well being. I met other patients who were far less fortunate than me; the very sick, the elderly and those who were simply coming to the end of their lives through failing health. Their ability to deal with the adversity the system threw at them was inspiring in itself. I came to strongly believe that it should not be necessary for these people to have to endure the dismay, the lack of respect, the poor facilities, the bad medical decisions and often the complete lack of communication and organisation within and between the departments. I heard whinging and moaning amongst NHS staff throughout my stay. It was mostly about them, their pay, the time they had off work, their day to day annoyances, their inadequate facilities and their day to day problems. They were all fit and healthy and going home each day to see their families and therefore escape the crazy circus they worked in. My inmates and fellow patients were not going home, yet hardly ever complained and put up with so much when they were already disadvantaged as a result of their failing health. They showed more respect and humility to the staff than was ever shown back and yet remained humble and courteous throughout. 'Thank you' was used at every opportunity. I clearly remember one Nurse saying to me on one occasion, "I can never understand why you keep thanking us, it's just our job. We should be doing this without thanks.' It concerned me as a statement at the time, as I had up to that point hoped that they realised we were bloody grateful to not be dying and that there was someone who could look after us in our time of need. We all hoped it wasn't just a job. I, of course, met competent and caring staff too. What I learnt from them was their growing frustration with the environment they worked in and the difficult situations they had to manage. There is no wonder when you see the organisation first hand that it is so difficult to achieve good staff retention within the NHS.

Everyone I speak to seems to be able to recount a tale about the NHS, often of dismay and disappointment, sometimes, but rarely, about their satisfaction, and of course inevitably about the life saving and intrinsic role it provided them and often society in its hour of need. Whatever the circumstances, it is almost always with a passionate viewpoint of their experience. Very often, and because of the situation they have been through, they have had to shout very loud indeed to be heard despite whatever outcome they experienced. This is a story for everyone who has had a similar time whilst dependent upon the NHS for their care and well being. It's a story particularly for anyone who has suffered inflammatory bowel disease or any similarly embarrassing conditions and struggled with the relative indignation. It's a story for everyone with an interest in the NHS who hopes to learn something from it. Part of my inspiration to write this account was my dear grandfather who died in the same hospital I found myself in. He went in with emphysema and died of an infection a few weeks later. I will never forget the indignity that such a wonderful man suffered at the end of his life. He stood over 6 feet tall, was strong, handsome and proud. He fought and served through the entire Second World War in campaigns in France and Africa. He sailed with the BEF in 1939 as a captain in the Royal Artillery. He fought defensive actions back to the beaches. He rowed off the beach and led his men to safety after several days of bombardment on the dunes. He was a distinguished yet modest man who rarely spoke of his achievements. He was great fun and excelled at sports, particularly rugby and golf, which he played to scratch. He achieved all sorts of new ideas in business and was forward thinking. He loved his family and was very dear to all of his grand children. He was thought about in a very high regard by everyone who knew him. By the end he resembled a shell of the man we knew. He suffered dreadfully towards the end. Each time we went in to see him he complained about the food, the lack of cleaning, the lack of care and the lack of respect shown to him by the staff. At the time we thought he was making it up and that it couldn't be that bad. We put it down to grumpy old man syndrome and the huge chasm that existed between contemporary values and those he had established through his own life. I have subsequently learnt he was right. I guess we didn't shout loud enough for him.

At this point I will say little more. I have found that being too critical at such an early stage can be a risky business. Hospital staff can react quite badly to patient's opinions and in being admitted for an in growing toe nail you can find yourself transferred to the critical list for orthopaedic surgery and then wake up with pins in your ankles. I have heard so many nurses, doctors and managers defend their health service whether it be whilst I was in hospital, in newspapers or on talk shows. Jeremy Vine on Radio 2 recently had nurses calling to defend practices which were apparently sub standard according to other callers in meeting cleaning requirements in hospitals. The callers who were either ex patients or hospital visitors were claiming that the food industry had higher hygiene standards than the NHS. There is no smoke without fire and by my experience I would tend to agree. I know this is delicate territory but for those who wish to defend the NHS please read my story before deciding, as it is a true account. I know as well as anyone in the UK what a sterling job the NHS does day to day in maintaining and saving life in our country. I want to make sure that everyone benefits from the same high standard of care which enables these success stories to become reality. I am sure by the time you have finished reading my account that you will question what happened to me and others whilst I was ill, just as I have done.

I do hope today's politicians keep a copy of my story by their bedside so that they have a few nightmares whilst they sleep. It might then compel them into some form of useful action. Their recent pride in eradicating the £1/2 billion NHS deficit through cut backs will of course have done so much for their swollen Westminster pride and self opinion. It will have achieved nothing of course for patient care! When their dreams drift towards the fear of being treated in a badly run hospital, the fear of not knowing whether they might live or die, the thought of MRSA mutating as it creeps towards them over an unwashed floor, calling out in the night without any response from a nurse, simply because there is no one there, the loneliness in an A&E department whilst sat on a trolley, the dismissive frank news about your impending mortality from a detached consultant or the fear of putting your trust in a man with a knife whom you neither know nor respect, then each politician will be having the same terrifying and life altering dreams each patient has when they lay waiting in an NHS hospital, hoping their lives will improve.

I would have enjoyed the opportunity of delivering my tale to those who established the NHS, Atlee and

Bevan. I guess when they set the job up they had enormous aspirations to deliver incredible levels of consistent care to people who really mattered. After reading it, I wonder what they would think about their 'New Jerusalem'. Normal people seem to be treated inconsistently, particularly the elderly, who in my opinion deserve our greatest attention. I suspect it would be an eye opener in comparison to what they set up back in 1948.

Losing control.

One of the aspects of our lives we take for granted is the day to day control we have when we are healthy. We usually make hundreds of minor decisions every day which determine our regular activities and give us our sense of purpose and confidence. Even when we suffer from minor ailments and conditions it is unusual to lose that feeling of control. Indeed a recent fracture of the 5th and 6th ribs had done little to dent my growing ambition to emulate Richard Hill or Martin Corry when I played in the back row for the local Rugby Club's Veterans side on tour in November. In the past my health had generally been good; I had never been seriously ill although IBS had troubled me infrequently for 20 years and I had grown to learn to put up with it. In my opinion I had been lucky. I had never suffered from a disease or condition which took my control away. As a result I had never really understood what it meant to be trapped in a situation which required a total reliance upon other people's decision making abilities.

I had come through an extraordinary sequence of events in 2006. My marriage had collapsed under the strain of work and through us growing apart. My workload had increased within our family business through the same period. It was to such a point that I had worked from early February through to mid October without a single day off, often working 12 -18 hour days and running right through 24- 36 hours on several occasions. It was an unusual period but it was an extremely intensive and busy business which over the years had always demanded a huge amount of my attention. Farming had been through the toughest challenges it had faced for over 70 years. In order to survive, more and more effort had been required just to stand still. Our type of farming business was intensive anyway but with growth and integration with packing and delivery of our products too, there was an ever increasing workload which I knew I needed to address. The fact that I had stepped up another gear or two was less obvious to me than to some. I had been fortunate enough from mid January to early February to spend time with a group of likeminded Agriculturalists at Imperial College, Wye studying an advanced business management course. That one experience had made me evermore determined to implement change in my life to achieve a degree of work / life balance. As the year progressed I was fortunate to be put forward for a prestigious Farming Award which proved both enjoyable and inspiring. Off the back of my various experiences I had successfully applied for a Nuffield Farming Scholarship which was likely to turn into a lifetime opportunity during 2007. My relationship with my family business became untenable during the latter part of the year as it became clearer by the day that the changes I wanted to implement were non-negotiable and my opinion was in contrast to the other partners. I could feel a mounting pressure which I knew would have to be addressed at some stage. Rather than create any regrettable long term friction I made the decision to withdraw and look for opportunities outside the safety net of our family and business. It was one of the toughest decisions I had ever had to make. However once I had made it and been through the pain, I experienced a refreshing view about my future. I was 42, single and had the world at my feet. I felt great and so I was surprised by the sudden decline in my health. That my health was starting to suffer should have been no great surprise to me and I know others were concerned about me. I suppose the physical and emotional strains had been significant. However at this stage you do not question your sustainability on a physical scale. You constantly look forwards towards the solutions to your problems. This usually means stepping up a gear rather than down, as change and new challenges require additional effort to achieve them. However if your health isn't secured the targets become unobtainable.

It was January 15th, two days away from my final London interview which would act as a portal to a very exciting 2007 with a trip to Calgary at the end of February followed by a whole 18 months of potential exploration mixed with a new career direction. I had never been more excited about an opportunity in my entire life. The Nuffield Scholarship had come at a time when there was a combination of inspiration, need and ability as well as a desire to deliver something back to the Industry which had served me so well over the last 20 years. I had spent months thinking about it and weeks preparing. Over the last two weeks I had revised various important issues, studied current affairs avidly, fine tuned my area of interest and honed my interview skills. I was as ready as I could be and tomorrow morning I would be boarding a train down to London where I was to stay with family in preparation for my early appointment in Bedford Square the next day.

That day started normally. I hadn't felt unwell beforehand. My previous weekend had been pretty normal. I had been out at a friend's house on Saturday at an excellent dinner party where I enjoyed myself on a par with everyone else. Sunday had been a typical day of late. A walk, a bit of work, the Sunday papers and the hint of a hangover. Monday had arrived and I felt as well and as normal as any other day. I had eaten a light breakfast that morning and was expecting an engineer to attend to my landrover discovery to fit a new hands free kit for my mobile phone. It's truly amazing.

If you want a new hand's free kit because your old one has packed up, you have to buy a new phone as well as a hands free kit. You can't obtain a replacement hands free kit because they become superseded and so once you have a new phone you have to then get the new hands free kit. What seemed like a cheap replacement phone soon had another £100 banged on it to fit the kit. I remember the engineer turning up. "Can you sit in your vehicle please, I need to check everything works" I climbed in and fiddled with the ignition and the switches so that he could check he wasn't going to be held liable for any of his potential incompetence. He sneezed and then leant across to me and in his fluent Hull accent declared, "By, I've got a rotten cold; I don't feel right well." "Oh sorry mate, you've probably got it now" "Terrific" I thought, "just what I need for an Interview and when did you assume you were my mate?" I left my vehicle in his hopefully competent hands hoping he might stick his fingers into the cigarette lighter and electrocute himself.

At about this time I started feeling chilled. You know, one of those moments when you feel like a ghost has walked behind you. I shivered horribly. A chilling frightening and back bone wriggling sort of feeling. I also realized I needed to go to the room which has the enormous pile of magazines which are periodically flicked through. As I sat reading about whether biogas from methane fermentation may be the next energy source of the future, I experienced a passing of wind of historical importance. Its volume and odour created a significant enough gap in the ozone layer to melt the Greenland ice cap in a matter of hours without any help from our industrialised civilisation. In swift succession, there followed what one would expect, in combination with what one wouldn't. My body spat out a dark gelatinous red bloody mess. I looked at it and being in my typically positive mood deducted a simple haemorrhoid. And so it continued through the morning with regular trips to the loo and becoming the world's expert on haemorrhoid diagnosis. It never occurred that it might be something more important or sinister and since I was by 2.30pm a leading consultant in the field of gastroenterology I clearly needed no second opinion. As the day progressed I failed to keep up, regressing in to a slightly insular, less confident and increasingly concerned keeper of the smallest room.

My ageing Labrador who at 15 years of age had recently shown a fine example of incontinence was now being led by example as I spent hourly trips to the loo dispersing what had now turned into a liquid magi mix type solution of the dark red variety. The dog which invariably liked to spend its time lying in the hall had evacuated itself behind closed doors so as to avoid the ever increasing stench emanating from her owner. By evening conditions had not improved and I had failed to eat anything else through the day. I was beginning to look pale and gaunt, resembling an ageing rocker following a 24 hour drugs and drinks binge without of course any of the upside. At this stage I was thinking about calling the cavalry. However I knew if I did, it would open a can of worms of python proportion and that there was little chance of ever getting the lid back on. Nonetheless expecting several informed opinions from my pharmacist sister, my very caring mum and my well informed dad I made a call home to report in that eldest son was going through some different experiences of late. I immediately refused a Helicopter, the services of Harley street surgeons, the ambulance or being rushed into A& E by various members of the family, some of which I'm sure were abroad at the time anyway and generally played down my condition minute by minute in an attempt to lend some reality to the situation. Retrospectively it would have been more sensible to have gone with the flow. This was the first denial of my loss of control. I really didn't want this, whatever it was, to happen. I had no idea, despite the recent diploma in gastroenterology what was happening to me and at 42 years of age self respect and independence are quite strong force fields in resisting interference in your life.

My second denial came about after calling NHS direct. The person on the other end of the phone had a very strong regional accent and clearly hadn't been living in Britain for long. I really struggled to understand exactly what she was saying. I think she found my Lincolnshire lilt tricky too. I did ask her which country she was actually in as I was concerned I had a call centre on the other side of the world on the phone. She did assure me that she was sat in the UK. Once we had worked out what each of us was saying we started to make a bit of progress. However as I discussed my symptoms it became clear that we needed a colour chart as I went through various shades of red to describe my symptoms. After a lengthy debate about whether it was 'red like a grape or red like a plum or a tomato' and was there 'a little bit or a lot of blood' and 'did it arrive quickly or was it all of the time', the advice was to go to A&E if I couldn't arrange an appointment to see my doctor. I was fairly unimpressed with the lack of technical ability of my NHS direct assistance. I guess if I had been suffering with a cold they might have been able to help. I tried the local surgery. Funnily enough the surgery was shut, but an answer phone declared I could call another number if it was an emergency. It was about as much help as going to the doctor and asking for something for persistent wind and him prescribing a kite. I tried the number and got an answering service. I didn't bother leaving a message. Regrettably I had decided I was not an emergency and so I didn't call the emergency number again. Retrospectively this was a mistake but at the time I was very conscious of not escalating the condition to 'emergency' proportions. I didn't want to be melodramatic or waste people's time if I wasn't seriously ill.

Over the last 20 years I had suffered from IBS, a common enough complaint in modern society. Sometimes you feel great and other times you have terrible painful cramps. Often your bowel habits are all over the place and you can feel tired and generally unhappy. The few occasions I had investigated it further through consultants and procedural examinations nothing had turned up to indicate it was anything other than IBS. I had turned into just another IBS statistic and whilst I was never happy with the diagnosis, I put up with it as there wasn't another option. Now partly as a result of all of the other eminent trainee gastroenterologists in my family who had recently contacted me on five minute intervals from throughout Lincolnshire I was beginning to think that this recent episode may be connected to my underlying IBS condition. Even so I remained tucked up in bed as I was sure my symptoms would improve. Well, they do, don't they? In all seriousness part of my reluctance to take it all to the next stage was undoubtedly my past experience with IBS. It is one of those conditions which comes and goes. You go from acute pain to normal living within 24 hours. I couldn't remember the countless occasions when I had felt dog rough and then slowly over a day I would recover to a semblance of normality. Sometimes it was diet, sometimes stress but most of the time no one had any idea at all what caused the episodes. Something in the deepest core of my memory banks was however beginning to acknowledge that this was not comparable to anything I had experienced before.

By 10.30pm I had started to feel distinctly unwell. I had a feeling of dread crawling all over me. It was as if my body was trying to communicate a message to explain that there was something seriously wrong and that I needed to be less heroic and more self preserving in my approach.

My episodes to the loo had now enabled me to practise a sprint start on a 15 minute interval. My record to date had been a full turn round from bed to loo, full baton hand over and back again in less than 2 minutes. It all depended on how much of the bloody foul mixture exited my body in one sitting. Each time I had to make a visit I analysed the situation, "Look it's just a motion; it's just a funny colour; it's not blood; you are going to be fine." I tried to convince myself. But as each episode ensued, the blood content increased and by midnight it was obvious to even a now veteran trainee gastroenterologist, my activity was far from normal. I had begun to rationalise the loss of blood in amounts. I concluded that I must be losing about 100mls of blood each time, so in an hour about a half a litre. I knew the human body held about 5 litres of blood. What I didn't know was how fast it regenerated the blood it lost. In addition within my calculations it was difficult to analyse how much was blood and how much was something else. On the basis that I was probably regenerating at least half of what I lost I was likely to run out of blood in about 10 hours. I was thinking by then that I could be starring in an episode of Holby City. It was all becoming a bit scary.

At about this point my brain went into overdrive. Adrenalin initiated by fear kicked in and I suddenly found I had a million ideas roaring around in my head. Worryingly I started talking to myself. I tried to rationalise the situation and analyse what was happening to me. I realised I was seriously ill. It suddenly dawned on me that I might not be going to London and that I was going to miss my opportunity of a lifetime. I felt gutted. For a while I went in to denial. I repeatedly told myself that I wasn't ill; this was my moment in time; I was going to recover; I was going to make the Interview somehow. Pigs flew didn't they? Any flies on the wall would have seen a scared sorry looking figure with his hands clasped around his legs and his chin on his knees rocking gently and quietly debating the pro's and con's of his dodgy reality.

Unfortunately by 00.20am my condition had deteriorated further. The time between episodes had shortened to 10 minutes and more fluid rushed from my body each time. I remember standing up after a particularly obnoxious session, the stench was consuming. I felt utterly miserable. I looked into the bathroom mirror thinking that an intruder had somehow crept in to the bathroom as a complete stranger looked back at me. A pale, wrinkled, hollow face peered from my reflection. It was at this moment that I realised I could no longer afford to pretend my health was not at risk. I could hear my sister's pharmaceutical advice ringing in my ears to get to a hospital. I remembered the NHS direct advice – get to A&E. I could hear my mother from 26 miles away declaring my incomprehensible stupidity for not already being in a Harley Street Clinic via air ambulance 12 hours ago. I knew they were all right. Before I could leave the bathroom another bout of fluid left my body. It was liquid, dark red, foul smelling and like a torrent. An Orc would have been proud of it, but I didn't much feel like auditioning for Peter Jackson. It felt like all of my dreams were being dashed. I was being purged of this hell fluid in repentance to some terrible deed that the almighty had deemed worthy of such suffering. I couldn't remember doing anything that bad though.

I unexpectedly found myself praying and asking for help and forgiveness. I felt guilty I hadn't been to church much recently and guessed I was at the back of a long queue. I prayed a bit harder but it didn't seem to change much. Since I had not recently shown a great deal of interest in my spirituality I realised that maybe my condition was rather more serious than could be sorted by my sudden reliance on the good lord that very minute and I was so very scared knowing even he couldn't help me. Like the last piece of a jigsaw falling in to place a light went on in my brain that I needed a doctor very quickly. I also suddenly realised I had lost control.

Stars.

It was decision time and I needed to get to hospital? I just couldn't decide whether I should call an ambulance, get hold of a family member or even drive myself in? I just couldn't see myself justifying the full Casualty paramedic experience and since it was now into the wee hours I felt troubled by expecting someone else to drive miles out of their way to take me in to hospital. Right or wrong, I started looking for the car keys. I hadn't quite got the jet engine strapped to my back in Richard Hammond fashion, but I was sure I could make it safely and in quicker time by setting off myself and as soon as possible. If I waited for either an ambulance or a friend I would lose valuable time and I was suddenly feeling desperate. I quickly dressed, throwing on what I had worn earlier the day before which lay by the bed in a crumpled heap, grabbed my mobile phone and went downstairs. My faithful 15 year old Labrador lay on her nest looking up at me with her big brown eyes. Her health had also recently taken a turn for the worse and she was suffering from old age and a troubling infection. I squatted down next to her, rested my hand on her head and said goodbye. "Well, Bramble I really hope we see each other again soon" I bent over and kissed her head and there was the merest wag of a tail. I'll get Sandra to come and look after you," I promised her. Sandra was my stalwart whenever I needed a bit of pet sitting. I unlocked the door and went outside into a beautiful clear night full of stars. Halfway to the land rover I realised that I wasn't going to be making the hospital soon and dashed back in to alleviate myself of what I thought must be becoming a valued commodity in my body. How much blood did Hancock determine was held in one arm? I noticed I was starting to get a bit panic stricken. My mind was starting to race and I realised I probably wasn't in the best condition to drive. However I felt as though I was committed to my cause and that I shouldn't deflect from my objective, tricky as it might turn out to be. In a rather agricultural fashion I grabbed some kitchen roll for the inevitable interruption to my imminent mercy dash, very nearly tripped up over the now inquisitive Bramble and after locking the door ran to my land rover. Once sat in it I wished I had an emergency type beacon and siren. Nonetheless the Land rover immediately evolved Ferrari F1 abilities and I was on my way breaking the speed limit through the village. As I left the village outskirts I saw a fox cross the road. It was the first of seven foxes I was to see on my 12 mile journey. Each one crossed the road in front of me, left to right, in some sort of surreal repeat which tested and questioned my perception of reality each time it happened. I have never seen so many in one journey and at times I thought I was hallucinating. My senses throughout the journey were heightened anyway. I was aware of the colours, the sky, the stars, people's houses, who still had lights on. It was like I was taking it all in because it all felt more important than usual. A mounting pressure in my bowels suggested that before too much longer and well before I made the hospital I would need to give up more of my precious blood. My mind suddenly filled with some of the most negative thoughts I had encountered in the experience to date. "What if I've left it too late?", "What if I don't make the hospital?" I was driving past one of the Farm's I had managed for several years and I knew that a field entrance was coming up. I assumed the need for a Grand prix pit stop. No refuelling or tyres for me but make sure the pit crew have got full protective clothing on as this might be messy. I leapt out of the car grabbing the kitchen roll and padded in to the field. I hadn't seen another car on the road and with my engine switched off the silence was deafening. I looked up into the sky at a display of bright brilliant stars and felt very insignificant indeed.

Remembering that I was a farmer in a country of burdensome over regulation and that there was some issue with applying blood to fields I aimed in the direction of the hedge bottom hoping that there were no stinging nettles to add insult to injury. I stayed there for a while. Conscious of the 10 minute journey I had remaining, I didn't fancy exploring the possibilities of repeating the experience in Mrs Jones's garden 5 miles down the road heading in to town. I suddenly realised I had failed to let anyone know where I was. Crouched amidst my farming, with my trousers around my ankles and a star studded sky above me I frantically sent texts to the nearest and dearest about my intended destination. As I sent the texts I wondered how they might consider receiving a message "Heading in to Hospital tonight. Internal bleeding. Talk soon." It was only in the middle of December that I had experienced a minor operation. It had required 48 hours in a private hospital and had gone so smoothly my self-belief in the health service was at an all time high. I had almost forgotten it had ever taken place even though it was only a month ago to the day. As I wrote and sent the texts I realised they would all assume it was another bit of me that was bleeding, the bit I had been operated on, but I couldn't find the enthusiasm to change and resend the text and since most of the family were now trainee gastroenterologists I was sure they would sort out any confusion. I looked up at the stars in the sky. It was a sky full of stars and as clear a night as I could recently remember. It reminded me briefly of a wonderful gag Les Dawson used to tell and which always made me smile; "As I watched the waxing moon ride across the zenith of the heavens like an amber chariot towards the ebon void of infinite space wherein the tethered belts of Jupiter and Mars hung forever festooned in their orbital majesty, I thought I must put a roof on this lavatory!" My mind was snapped back to the reality of the situation as I lost a bit more blood and a cold clammy feeling crept over me, a thought crept across my tired and worried mind, "I hoped I wasn't going to die! I so hoped not as there was still far too much to do."

Despite my newly acquired morbidity, I realised that it was now or never and as I was feeling very cold I climbed back into the land rover and headed for the hospital. "I didn't want to die; I wasn't going to die". I so wanted it be at a ripe old age jumping about with a woman forty years younger than me or stood in a river with a rod in my hand trying to land a record salmon. I really didn't want the indignity of being found with my trousers around my ankles in a field covered in blood. I repeated back to myself three or four times, "Not going to die, not going to die!". As I hit the empty dual carriageway and the speedometer tickled 90mph I was really hoping for the flash of blue lights and a police escort. It would be the one time in your life when you might expect a conciliatory response from a traffic cop. As I drove in to town I slowed down and obeyed the speed limit. I suddenly remembered how long it took through town at 30 mph to reach the hospital. By this stage I had seen 4 foxes and I was to see a further 3 as I drove through urban Lincolnshire. "Tally Ho!" I thought. Just as long as I don't have to jump any hedges and bare my behind to the local residents I didn't mind how many foxes crossed my path.

After an age I pulled in to the hospital car park, collected my parking ticket at the barrier and found somewhere to dump the land rover. After a very quick check that there was nothing worth nicking out of it I walked quickly over to A& E reception holding my bowels.

I was conscious of how I looked and remember trying to straighten my bed head as I approach the kiosk. Making a good first impression is of course so important. However I felt like a freak; pale, dishevelled, dirty, ill and very tired. "Hello, excuse me. "The three ladies sat behind the counter remained in avid debate about what Jim had said to Kev. They wouldn't have been out of place in the Rovers Return in the window bay sat round a pint and a sweet sherry. "Sorry, excuse me" I repeated. "Yes luv, what do you want? "Having grabbed their attention," I'm admitting myself in to A & E". "Name luv?" And so over the next few minutes I gave up my details and my address to find out that I was on the register which was comforting. "You are Charles Davey? " "No, Edward, but my first name is Charles" "What's the problem?" "I seem to have an internal bleed" "Oh dear, what did Jim say Dawn? Sorry luv, with you in a tic. Ok?" she said barely acknowledging me. I actually thought, "No, not bloody ok actually." I thought about how I had looked in the bathroom mirror before I had left home and wondered how I looked now. Maybe I was ruddy faced as if I had spent the afternoon on the sea front or tanned and toned after two weeks in Bermuda, but I bloody well doubted it. I was never asked how I felt, never asked if I felt ill or was in danger of needing a nurse quite quickly. It was 00.50 am. How many people at this time in the morning looking like I did admit themselves to an A&E department declaring an internal bleed? I thought it would have been worth at least a cursory question of my health status. There was no one about, other than a man standing outside the main doors smoking. There was no queue, no people needing emergency assistance. In fact apart from the three of them, two having fallen back into their concern regarding

Jim and Kev, there was no one other than the smoker and me in evidence. "Ok luv, take this form round to the nurse's station and ring the bell once. Someone will come to see you. So Kev reckoned what Dawn?" I thanked her although it was clear she didn't hear me, took the form and walked in to the A&E waiting room which was completely empty. My immediate reaction was that at least I would be seen quickly.

Signage in hospitals is never good. Firstly there are too many, secondly they are confusing and thirdly hospitals are like rabbit warrens. In my opinion there should be two, one saying "In" and one saying "Out". Trying to find a sign 6" square next to a door wasn't as easy as it had sounded. Nonetheless after a little bit of wandering down a wrong corridor I found the sign, "Press bell once and wait!" I did as I was asked and waited. After a couple of minutes I realised that waiting wasn't an option as I needed to bleed in to the hospital facilities rather urgently. As luck would have it the nearest loo was only yards away from the sign. I rushed in, lost some blood, tidied myself up a bit and came back to wait next to the sign. A thought occurred to me. "What if I had missed the nurse?" Did I need to press again or would this constitute some flagrant abuse of rule 2.1a part 7 sub section c on bell ringing. I rang it anyway, twice. I could feel myself flinching expecting the irate thought police to appear and reprimand me for unnecessary abuse of the bell. 5 minutes passed and nothing happened. Somewhere in the background behind doors I could hear people and activity but none of it seemed to be getting any nearer to me. Waiting again became an issue and I darted back in to lose more valuable blood. I was feeling incredibly tired, cold and a bit light headed. I began to wonder if you saw stars when you fainted as in the cartoons. I tried to picture the stars I had seen earlier to take my mind off the situation I found myself in. I rang the bell again with as little result as before, but by now I couldn't give a toss if anyone didn't like it. I gave it another bash. Having stood near the bell for 15 minutes I decided I might as well be sat down and walked back the dozen or so yards in to the A&E waiting room. The room had a ceiling with large strip lights and as a result devoid of any warmth or character. A series of 40 or so plastic seats were set out in the room. The only one that was occupied was mine. At least it wasn't busy and I thought I would get seen quickly. Opposite me against the wall sat a drinks and snacks dispenser. Every unhealthy can of sugar intoxicating fizzy drink and every fattening piece of chocolate imaginable sat in rows staring at me. I sat clutching my form, alone, tired, scared and slightly concerned that if someone didn't see me soon I might slip the surly bonds of earth in this miserable plain non descript uncared for room. I suddenly felt unwell again and I stood up and headed for another bout of blood loss and hell fluid.

Once I was seated again and in my lonely vigil of the drinks dispenser I contemplated my predicament. Should I ring the bell again; shout; open doors; go back to reception? I had walked through the main doors at 00.50 am. It was now 1.20 am. I had been to the loo three more times and I was no further to seeing a nurse than going to London for my interview. I stood up and walked to the bell. I rang it twice, knocked on a couple of doors and called "Hello?" No response. Either they had a coach crash to deal with, or they had all cleared off down to the pub. Maybe aliens had abducted the entire A&E team. No one appeared. I stood and waited hopefully for a while and then realised another trip was required. I walked in to the Loo for the fourth time and for the first time really took notice of it. The hand towel bin was overflowing and the spent damp paper towels were cascaded across the floor. The taps at the sinks had lost their tops so cold couldn't be differentiated from hot. The loo door lock didn't work and there was paper and grime around the toilet on the floor. There was no compliance sign saying this toilet had been checked by staff and deemed acceptable which was so often found in at least a fuel station lavatory. I suddenly felt exposed to the environment I was in. My skin crawled at the prospect of being dependent on these facilities. They were suddenly a long way from the comforts of home. I was feeling frighteningly unwell. After washing my hands for the twentieth time that day I walked out of the loo and rang the bell again. As if by magic an Asian doctor appeared immediately through the door. However as she was about to walk past me I said, "excuse me, I have been asked to give you this. I seem to be bleeding internally." " Ok" she said, "Take a seat I will be with you shortly." I felt like saying "you must be bloody joking or have you had a nice time down the boozer?" I wanted to be seen ASAP. I wanted someone to show me some care and attention. I didn't make a habit of admitting myself to an A & E in the middle of the night. However as alienating the first medical staff I met didn't seem appropriate, I said nothing and walked back to take up my dispenser vigil. None of the drinks or chocolate bars had escaped. I didn't fancy anything from the dispenser myself as apart from feeling ill I also felt faint. However at least I wasn't seeing stars, yet.

Fish and Chips.

I wasn't surprised when the Doctor failed to return. Although I had already started to form an opinion about the services I was experiencing and they weren't good, I wasn't starting to panic. During my stay I was to meet 10 different doctors, a registrar or two and various consultants. Keeping them numbered was the only way I could keep track of their chronology. Doc 1, a young Asian lady doctor, had seemed confident and competent enough. It just seemed strange that she hadn't come back and I wondered whether I should have made more fuss. According to Tony Blair, A&E is the shop window of the NHS and so I guess one should have expected a degree of quality in the standards of staff within this department. The fact that she left me there didn't at the time concern me unduly as I assumed she had a system. Maybe she always read the admission form sat at her desk or maybe she still had a life threatening issue to deal with behind a closed door. I didn't know and I certainly didn't want to cause any problems. Nonetheless I felt very poorly and I knew that unless someone took charge very soon I would become a much more urgent case in the not too distant future. I knew I had lost a lot of blood and I felt weaker by the minute. I felt very light headed and I still visited the now well known and rather incompliant loo outside the A&E department every 10 minutes.

I had become aware of the noise of chatter somewhere nearby for a while now. It reminded me of the prattle of people who work together and know each other well. I couldn't make out particular conversations or hear exactly what was said. However occasional laughter interrupted people talking over each other and it was clear staff were congregated somewhere quite near. I assumed it might be a meeting or possibly a break. Everyone needs one of those. I assumed that if it was a break, a well organised A&E department would be running a shift basis to cover patient's requirements and that there would be someone to see me soon.

It was with great relief that the A& E department doors were pushed open by a young attractive dark haired nurse in her scrubs. She saw me and smiled. I could feel my bum lifting off the seat, not because of its next emission but in anticipation of a greeting from this vision of care. However within yards of reaching me she turned sharp left and stood in front of the drinks dispenser. Apart from the weak smile I had received there was no further recognition, no salutation and no conversation. I fell back in to the chair and felt confused. I thought "It hadn't been Doc 1, so probably this wasn't the right person anyway." I decided that rather than confuse the issue I should wait for Doc 1's return. I waited. "Bloody thing" the nurse declared. "For fuck's sake." Having put her money in to the dispenser the machine wasn't playing ball. She gave the dispenser a kick and my opinion of her and the department dipped. "I bloody hate it when this happens." I wasn't sure if she was talking to me or just ripping into the inanimate object before her. I didn't much feel like entering a debate about the unreliability of a drinks dispenser and so remained painfully silent. After a series of further expletives she bent over and proceeded to reach through the bottom flap with her arm and tease the offending bottle away from its hanger. She shook the machine whilst grappling inside and swearing under her breath that she just couldn't believe it. Nor could I. I was left with a view of a not unattractive blue clad arse shaking in rhythm to her attempts to extricate the bottle. I couldn't help thinking that if she was ever to conduct an assist at a difficult birth there would be every chance of a prolapse. Finally and with the dignity of a Mariner's football supporter experiencing a goal, she exalted as she turned, "Thank fuck for that, these machines are a pain in the arse." As again I wasn't clear whether I was expected to join in I sat there rather bemused and nodded like a fool. She walked past me and towards a door from where a growing volume of noise was building. With her successful booty in her hand she opened the door. As it opened I was hit by a cacophony of spirited noise comparable to a bar at 11pm and the smell of fish and chips. Someone had been down to the chippy and as far as I could make out the entire A & E department were sat in this room devouring their evening shift treat. I was appalled. I had assumed every A & E department should smell of antiseptic and be full of the sounds of quiet medical efficiency, crisp crackling linen and monitor noises. It was more like a night out on the town. My confidence dipped again. In combination with my declining health, my psychological well being seemed to be under threat. My instinctive feeling was to run. I had a phrase running through my head "Fear, Fire, Foes, - Flee". Should I get back in to my land rover and drive to another hospital? One was about thirty five minutes away. Somehow I kept my bum on a seat. It was 1.35 am. I felt terrible and scared. Who was I about to put my trust in? I girded my loins. There were people in far worse situations than this, I assured myself. Keep your head and get on with it, I told myself. You are in the right place, I convinced myself. But even as the thought passed through my mind I didn't really believe it. My shoulders sagged, I put my head in my hands and I sat and felt utterly miserable. It was only the need to get up and lose some more blood that galvanised me into any form of action. On my return from another whirlwind of activity I was beginning not to care. The thought of dying in isolation in a desperately lonely A & E waiting room returned. However the irony of such a possibility made me smile. When the problem is usually a minimum 4 hour wait because of the concentration of bodies filling these now empty seats, it was comical that I could be sat here alone for the best part of an hour bleeding. I was amazed that now having met two members of the A & E team I still hadn't been asked if I was ok. I was bleeding, I was the sole occupant of the A & E waiting room, I looked ghastly. Maybe I needed a sign around my neck "THIS IS A PATIENT". The fact that the A & E staff were stuffing their faces seemed incredible. I couldn't imagine "speeding up one's consumption of fish and chips" being used regularly by Tony Blair as a debating point to reduce waiting times in A & E departments. It felt like a sketch out of the Fast Show. I chuckled to myself and hoped that somewhere someone was looking down on me and that intervention of a heavenly nature might work in my favour. Maybe someone might come and offer me a chip.

I sat and patiently waited as patients do. I was disappointed with what had happened to me so far. I knew people had to wait for hours to be seen sometimes. Even so I had a gastric bleed and I was the only person to be seen in the department's waiting room. I guess if I'd stopped off at the chippy on the way in and bought everyone haddock and chips I would already be under observation from the A&E department, probably with salt and vinegar soaked fingers.

I noticed that the noise had reduced at the Chippy. Doc 1 appeared through the main swing doors of the A& E department. "Mr Charles Davi?" I couldn't find the energy to explain that I preferred "Edward" and that I had been called Edward since week 1 of my life, my surname was Davey and not even my enemies called me Charles, so I answered "yes".

Wayne and Waynetta.

Doc 1 held the door open for me, I ducked under her arm and I walked into the A & E department. Once I was past the nurse's station there were various half drawn curtains. An occasional trolley was parked up behind some of the curtains, although most were empty. We walked to the far end of a room which was no more than 20 metres long. On one side of a passageway created by a wall to the left and various curtains to the right, there were small treatment bays. An odd one appeared occupied but there was no obvious urgency within the department. The staff seemed to outnumber the sick people by 3 to 1. However one trolley had a curtain partly pulled around it and there were two chairs pulled up next to the trolley occupied by two cases for the obesity ward. Before them lay an elderly lady who was either asleep or unconscious. If they had been my visitors, I would have preferred unconscious. Opposite this curtained bay and on the other side of the passage, a recess resembling a broom cupboard awaited me. "Just sit here" Doc 1 told me and I duly obliged. As I rested on the edge of a trolley which left about 3 feet between it and the wall of the broom cupboard I realised it wouldn't be long before I would have to dart back down the department. I needed to take my mind off things. My attention was drawn to the partly opened curtain opposite me. There was a most interesting conversation which drifted out of it emanating from the two rather large people sat next to the trolley bed. "Wanna a crisp?" "Nah, gir us some of that pizza," she rasped. Her 40 a day habit sounded like it was impacting a bit. The view of an enormous builder's bum was nearly enough to put me into cardiac arrest. I seemed to have been left in the public bar of "The Grim Reaper pub." There was I thinking I was in an A & E department. "I don't reckon it were that bad you know" the enormous cleft commented. "It weren't so much racialism as she were just fed up with the others" "Yeah, I'd ate it if I ad to spend time with people that I didn't know." I suddenly realised I was being entertained by Wayne and Waynetta Slob and their view on the Jade Goody debate. "Pass us the coke will ya." I couldn't take my eyes off the scene before me. The elderly grey haired relative lay motionless on her trolley. Waynetta, sat in her coat, dug into her carrier bag and pulled out more of their picnic. Wayne just kept winding his food in. I felt very very sorry for the poor elderly lady. "It were really funny when she come out and didn't know nothing about it." "Yeah, the look on her face." "That booing really got her." I began to wonder whether the poor old lady laid out in front of them was in fact a relative at all. Maybe since Big Brother had finished and instead of watching it on the TV, they had come down to A & E to enjoy "Reality Suffering, the show where you get to choose who suffers the most! Sit by your victim, snacks available. Get a two for one, yes there's another one across the aisle if the first one isn't moving much!"

Before I could further enjoy the banter from the ghoulish and inexpedient guests of the "Grim reaper" I was interrupted by Doc1. Fortunately she provided a wonderful screen and blocked off the view to the cod head's crack. "Ok, please can you tell me what the problem is?" "Well, I'm losing a lot of blood and have been for a while." Unfortunately by the time I had made this initial statement I realised I had to apologise and retreat back down the department again. I was delighted to find that by now my case was deserving of some sympathy. The nurses stood behind the station desk actually looked at me, as like a boomerang I passed the desk to and fro to lose various quantities of hell fluid over the next ten minutes in 3 minute intervals. Each time I got back to my broom cupboard Doc I was there. The fact that she had decided to stick by me was reassuring. She asked me as many expedient questions as my journeying to and fro would allow and I began to realise that she was quite good at her job. I was even more impressed when on one occasion she reversed out of our broom cupboard and upon turning went in to shock at the sight of what lay across the passageway. She abruptly pulled the curtain to and in sympathy retorted, "That's the last thing you need to be looking at. What a sight! " By now I was connected up to monitoring equipment on a regular basis. Blood pressure, pulse, oxygen and temperature were regularly checked. I was sent off to retrieve a sample of the fluid which I had recently become so accustomed too. I didn't know whether to wave, strike up a conversation or just creep below the desk where the nurses congregated as my passing was becoming a minute by minute regular event. Upon my return Doc I took several blood samples. It seemed to take ages for her to find a suitable vein. It appeared that there was a problem with the availability of the red stuff. "Not exactly surprising," I thought. Hancock's trip to the blood donor recurred in my mind and I chuckled. Eventually after trying the back of both hands and each upper fore arm and after lots of strap tightening, fist clenching and a couple of abortive attempts, a trickle started running in to the syringe and vial. Once the bloods had been taken Doc I inserted a canula into my right hand and connected an IV drip. "Ok we are not sure what is happening at the moment. You appear to be losing some blood, but we don't know why. It could be a number of things." Doc I proceeded to investigate my last few hours and days. I was asked about reactions, allergies, previous illness, drugs and alcohol. It was 1.55 am. I was incredibly tired. I felt very ill. I wasn't sure whether I told her the correct information. I felt groggy and slightly disorientated. I half sat and half lay on the trolley. From across the way I heard Wayne offering his opinion on Shilpa Shetty as before me, Doc 1 shook her head in disbelief. I asked if I could go and lose some more red stuff. However I received a negative, no way, nope can do sort of response. It appeared that now I was connected up, it would have to come to me. It had never occurred to me until this point what that exactly meant. I imagined a mobile loo, or perhaps a chemical toilet. I thought I may be allowed a mobile drip and that my trolley would be near to a loo. My heart sank when Doc 1 returned with a piece of reinforced cardboard shaped like a potty. "Please use this" "Please can I go home" I thought, "I've had enough." "We need to see what's coming out," she stated. "My god, what are you people?" I thought. "Have you any idea how foul this stuff is? You may need to evacuate the entire hospital if this stuff stays above ground."

Whether the impending degradation of squatting on a piece of cardboard was the cause or plain old biology took a hand I shall never know but before I could find the energy to either object or perch, things took a turn for the worse. I suddenly felt very light headed. Disorientation and lack of mobility became big issues. As hard as I tried to retain control of my body I realised I was fighting a losing battle. I fell back on to the trolley. There was a sense of urgency around me. Doc 1 disappeared briefly. I lay there alone looking up at the bright strip light in the ceiling with my mind stripped clear of any thought. Within a few seconds two nurses appeared alongside a rather anxious Doc 1. "Ok, check his blood pressure again, quick." "Mr Davey, can you hear me? How do you feel? Lay him flat. "I didn't answer. I couldn't be bothered. "He's 90 over 50 and falling. Going Tachy. Let's get an ECG on him."

On the opposite side of the passage Wayne and Waynetta were peering around their curtain whilst eating their crisps. They had never expected a Bogof. Their prostrate relative was after all a bit boring and in comparison to my audition for an episode of casualty I guess there was no contest. .

A nurse pulled off my top, which in any other situation would have seemed like a magical moment and stuck ECG pads on to my chest. I started to bleep rather fast. It seemed my relentless supply of blood had dried up. Tony Hancock eat your heart out. "Blood pressure is still low and falling." I felt helpless and carefree. I knew I was taking a turn for the worse but it didn't seem to matter. The suffering up to this point had been considerably worse than how I felt now it was becoming more serious. I could sense the concern of the medical staff and I could see their urgency. But I really couldn't care less as I drifted off.

It lasted all of 10 to 15 minutes. I didn't remember a thing whilst I was out. By 2.10am I seemed to have stabilised. I haven't a clue to this day what they did to me. Probably nothing. I felt less dizzy and I became aware of my environment quite quickly. I heard grazing and grumbling from across the way as Wayne continued his supper. I was on my own in the broom cupboard. The machine next to my trolley appeared to be behaving. I could hear various conversations between the nursing staff from their station. They discussed break times, holidays, new admission forms, broken pods and what Julie said to Dawn. It seemed patient care wasn't high up on the agenda as there was clearly a lot to moan about. Considering everything I had experienced to date they weren't doing much for my confidence. Despite my previous self assurance that I was in the right place I remained unconvinced. My spirits were low; I was confused and a little scared.

I realised that I needed to use the cardboard. I didn't much feel like getting up though. After what seemed an age and after various conversations in my head about the merits of my potential success in trolley gymnastics I slowly lifted myself up. It took far longer than normal to get in to a firing position. As I let go with the sound of a cow that had been fed on rotten stock feed potatoes I could only imagine the look on Wayne and Waynetta's faces. First the relative departmental quiet was shattered by intrusive bovine flatulence and then the invisible poisonous gas crept across the floor akin to mustard gas used on Flanders fields. I couldn't imagine anyone wanting to eat pizza after that. It wasn't long before a nurse appeared to find out who had let the cattle in to A & E and retrieve and dispose of the mix. I was utterly ashamed and embarrassed. Doc 1 turned up, immediately followed by Doc 2 both wrinkling their noses.

Doc 2 was again Asian, a little older, and I had the impression that he was more senior. There was a sense of déjà vu. He asked exactly the same questions as Doc 1. Name, Charles? Date of birth? When did I start feeling ill? What had happened? Any history of illness? Name of GP? Had I been drinking? Had I taken drugs? What colour was the blood? He asked me to explain the exact symptoms since I had started feeling ill and the timings of the various episodes. He showed concern and I began to feel as though maybe he would deliver the answers that had so far evaded Doc 1. I suspected at any moment to hear compassion in his voice. I hoped he would register the fearful state I was in. I felt scared. I knew nothing about my condition. I needed a degree of reassurance. From the questioning I started to assume that they thought I had somehow self abused or contracted this condition through mis-use of my body. I smelt, I was still losing blood and I knew this had never happened to me before in my entire life. I tried to convey my concerns to Doc 2. A Nurse squeezed back in to the broom cupboard and Doc I retreated towards Wayne and Waynetta. The nurse checked my obs. My blood pressure had made a slight recovery but was still down. The ECG was registering a more normal heart rate. Oxygen levels were recovering and my temperature was normal. "Mr Davey, are you in any pain?" That was the strange thing. Apart from the discomfort of passing the blood I had felt little pain at all. My abdomen had felt fairly normal. I realised that I must be a difficult case to diagnose. Although bleeding was evident, there was no visual sign to indicate from where and I had no distinct pain.

They didn't know me from Adam. All of the medical records about me would be on my GP's data base and not in this A & E departments files. For all they knew I could be an alcoholic, a drug addict and a liar. I guessed that sometimes they had to deal with all three. The fact that I was none seemed immaterial. As I lay thinking about what was happening to me I felt utterly exposed. I realised that unlike in an interview or at a meeting for which I was well prepared, conversation and first impressions had little bearing here. I had spent my recent past exploring my ability to impress my peers and here I was hardly able to string more than a few words together and of absolutely no help to these qualified doctors. I was alone and completely dependent upon the judgement of those now managing my case. I had no option but to trust them. It wasn't an easy decision.

After a few minutes analysing what he had learnt the doctor looked me in the eye. "You are losing blood from somewhere." My first impression of him was that I had a failed rocket scientist with inter planetary aspirations and back garden ability before me. "Your blood pressure is all over the place. We are going to take some more blood tests shortly – ok? The smell is an infection. We think you have dysentery." "Nurse, can you check his obs and then in a few minutes, another series of blood tests please." "I will see you later Mr Davey." With that Doc I & 2 disappeared. I can't say i was particularly inspired. I lay alone in my broom cupboard. So I had an infection. That's what this was all about, an infection! I felt partly relieved as the prognosis was probably good, but very dirty as I had a horrible infection. In my disorientated and dream like state I thought that I might just make London if I was better in the morning. I suddenly realised that the symptoms hadn't gone away and I reached for a fresh bit of cardboard. I didn't know much about dysentery other than it was very infectious. I guess eating next to a man with dysentery wasn't the greatest idea in the world. That didn't seem to bother Wayne, the nurses, Doc I or 2 or the rest of the NHS.

Angels.

When things are going against you or you are having a
bad patch, the smallest improvement seems a major step
forward. Usually out of all proportion you find yourself
grasping at the few positive things and try to build around
them. It's what keeps you sane in the darker moments. At
least that was what I found that particular night. A nurse
I hadn't seen before came in to the broom cupboard. She
smiled and it warmed my rather empty heart. She was
about my age, with neat blonde hair tied up in bunches,
a well pressed uniform and a happy disposition. From the
moment she walked in to the bay I knew she cared. She was
the first person I had met that actually focused on "caring."
"Hi, how are you doing?" I obviously didn't look very happy
or very well as before I could answer she carried on, "Oh,
love you are very poorly. Sorry but we need to get you
out of your things and in to a gown." "Once we have done
that, I will come back to take some more blood tests and
then we are going to move you to somewhere where I can
keep a better eye on you." Her very presence felt uplifting
and it felt like an angel had descended to care for me. She
left me alone to take off my few remaining clothes and pull
myself in to the revealing hospital gown. My indignity was
now complete, "Man wearing dress with dreadful bowel in
public area."

As I lay back down on the trolley my Angel returned
with a tray of needles and sample bottles. I was incredibly
thirsty. "Sorry love, you can't have anything to drink, but

don't worry, the IV will keep you topped up." She artfully extracted blood in a matter of seconds and I evolved the opinion that she was not only an angel but very good at her job too. Once she had dealt with the samples she was back again. "Right we are going to get you moved now." My thoughts were that by 2.30 am I was going to be put in an appropriate part of the hospital. I was going to begin receiving care from people just like the angel that had tidied around the trolley in anticipation of our move. She checked all of my belongings were bagged up and placed on my trolley and then checked I was ready too. I couldn't wait. To be away from Wayne and Waynetta would be relief beyond comprehension. To have some privacy so that I wasn't on public display would be very comforting. "Ok just before we go I want to check your obs again." She efficiently checks my blood pressure, pulse, oxygen and temperature. My blood pressure had dipped again but not as low as before and the ECG indicated a degree of normality. Once everything was stowed away the nurse pushed the trolley out of the broom cupboard. As I turned right my IV drip and various monitors flicked the curtain on the opposite side of the passageway revealing Wayne and Waynetta's night out. They looked up from their sandwiches with fascinated expressions. I felt like a reality TV character who had jumped through the screen into their front room and for the first time I could see the audience. They looked slightly bemused as I stared back at them and they quickly pulled their curtain back round. They had decided I might be contagious.

The trolley sped along the passageway for a further 8 yards and then stopped. I was looking up at the strip lights as I was put in to reverse. Within a few yards the nurse conceded that we had arrived. I had moved approximately 10 yards from my broom cupboard as well as Wayne and Waynetta. I peered forwards. I was slap bang in front of the nurse's station in the middle of A & E. "There you go." She explained. "Christ" I thought, "I'm in the middle of the bloody room. How on earth do I manage my recent bovine impressions parked here. I might as well be sat in the middle of Blundell Park with the floodlights on and a running commentary of my every activity." I clearly looked bewildered as without prompting, my Angel recognised my concerns. "It will be ok. We will draw a curtain round you and bring you a commode and some more inserts. Ok?" I couldn't find the enthusiasm to reply. I could not believe that I was to spend a period of time sat in the middle of the department with dysentery and as obnoxious a complaint as I was suffering from. Why not park me in the middle of the precinct or maybe on the Humber Bridge. Nonetheless she quickly wheeled in all of the fixtures and fittings required for a man in my condition. "How long will I be here?" "Not really sure love. There are no beds on wards available at the moment. You will need an isolation room so you will have to stay here for now. I will chase it though" she promised. She made sure I was comfortable. "Call me when you need it emptying" I shook my head. "Don't worry you'll know when it wants emptying." She departed through the now drawn curtain and returned to the nurse's station about 4 yards south of my feet. I could not believe a hospital in the 21st century didn't have the facilities to allow a patient some degree of dignity. I couldn't believe it could not provide at least a medically secure environment for a patient with an infection like dysentery. The noise of the night shift continued just a few paces away. "How do you fill in this form? I've not seen it before." "It's new, I think it's only just come on today." "It's bloody enormous, that's what it is. Have you seen this section at the back? I wouldn't have the first clue as to how to fill that in. Why have they changed it? Some smart arse somewhere with too much time on his hands! Here what's this bit; Have you seen this? I don't reckon this can apply to us we haven't got one of those, or those and what the hell is that. Might as well tear these up, what do you think?" And so it continued. Sometimes the conversations covered patient care, but usually they chatted about people, holidays, families and what A had said to B. It was a revelation and very different to my expectations of what an A & E department was meant to be about. There appeared to be none of the cut and thrust we are all conditioned to by watching 'Holby' or 'Casualty' on the TV. Admittedly I couldn't see anything, but I suspected that they were carrying out some functional tasks whilst they were talking. I so hoped they weren't leaning over the nurse's station like Les Dawson and Roy Barraclough in a 'Cissy and Ada' sketch. "Well you can say what you like but it's a funny looking baby to me. When was the last time you saw one with a cleft chin and two warts under its nose?" "You're looking at the wrong end!" "God, no wonder it didn't like it when I shoved it's dummy in." I tried to keep smiling as listening to their droning monologue made life even more dull than it had already become. It wasn't like they had many people to worry about as there were only 3 patients as far as I could work out in the department. The lady being visited by Wayne and Waynetta, another lady who had been wheeled in a while ago complaining of dizzy spells and yours truly made up the patient contingent. There appeared to be one doctor and about 5 nurses of one grade or another in and around the department. They spent the vast majority of their time sat at desks at the nurse's station filling in paperwork or writing communiqués to different departments. Nursing seemed to be a secondary occupation. I could hear people walking past the curtain at the end of my bed. They were so close that they could touch my feet if they put their arms through. I realised that despite my concerns I would have to perform within the facility provided. I was so pleased that the curtain was there. However sometimes when people walked past they caught it and it would begin to draw itself around. No one ever pulled it back and on these occasions I would be left exposed to the passing trade. To avoid detection I shuffled the commode as far from my bed as the IV would allow and perched precariously upon it. Blood, wind and Melina (and that's not a band from the 70's) arrived with a conviction. I climbed back on to the trolley as quickly as possible and waited for some attention. They must have heard me or seen me under the curtain. Surely now they must be able to smell me. Nobody came. Unbelievably the chatting had never stopped and as I listened hopefully I could hear the conversation drifting back to St. Lucia, Spain or Florida. "Oh I tell you that scuba diving was ace. I'm definitely going back. It was amazing, there was fish and all sorts and we went really deep after a week." I began to feel desperately lonely. I had for a moment believed I was going to be relieved of my indignity and moved to a more appropriate area; I had held some hope in my Angel delivering some form of minor miracle.

I lay on my trolley looking up at the strip light. It was so bright that even if I had wanted to try and sleep there was no way it would let me. I could feel the grittiness in my eyes registering with my brain that my body was very tired. I felt my recent optimism brought on by my angel's attention dissolve. Tears, so light I didn't register them at first, began to trickle down my face. Reality crashed in and for the very first time I knew that there was little chance of achieving any of my hopes and ambitions for 2007. The last 6 months had just been wiped out in that moment. All of the changes I had been through, the heart ache, the challenges and the effort that had gone in to enabling me to be ready for what lay ahead had been wasted. Bedford Square and my Interview were definitely off and I began to think that it may go further than that. I was desolate and lonely. A combination of the fear of the unknown and the self pitying realisation of what I had lost and how much of my life had contributed to this moment crippled my mind. My ambition and opportunity to achieve the Scholarship, travel the world and learn from the CEO's and MD's, the Government ministers and the Scientists, the farmers and the everyday people I might have met was gone. The enormous commitment to a separation from my beautiful wife and the significant sacrifices we had both made earlier last year seemed shattered in that instant. I had never missed her more since our split than at that moment. My ultimate and hard fought for decision to step back from a business I had committed every ounce of passion and determination I could afford over twenty years seemed wasted. My core principles and values of loyalty and trust which I had risked in order to take all of those decisions fell about in my mind as if they were in a tumble dryer. I found myself questioning whether it had all been worthwhile. It seemed cruel to deny myself some optimism and yet I was on a one way street to self pity city. I thought about the nice times I had recently enjoyed. The new people I had met on my journeys and the wonderful friends I had been fortunate to have support from through the rocky times. I promised myself that once I was better I was going to arrange a huge party and dance away through the early hours of the morning.

Logically, I tried to overcome the maelstrom of feelings charging around my head. It was as though I was never going to be allowed to justify many of the recent decisions I had made in my life, the successful outcomes of which would have reflected both the credibility of the decisions and my ability. In the one moment in my life when I had set out to achieve a degree of excellence and try to take a truly independent approach I found myself undermined by an essential building block in the whole concept, my health.

Unfortunately and whether I liked it or not I couldn't do much about my health at this stage without the medical fraternity. I tried to apply some rationality to my thoughts. I registered the emotion as a moment in time. I realised in the same instant that none of the people taking responsibility for me right now and who stood within a matter of a few feet of me had any concept of what was going through my mind. I tried drying my eyes but they wouldn't stop running. I had so wanted to enjoy the challenges of a lifetime and I was stuck on this bloody awful trolley. I clenched my jaw, wiped away the tears and became a little bit angry. "Nurse" I yelled. It was 3.00 am.

My Angel appeared and dealt with the commode efficiently and without fuss. From then on she appeared every 10 to 15 minutes. She repeatedly checked my obs, my drip, my ECG. She kept my commode clear just as regularly. I asked her to contact my relatives. She immediately went to the phone. I feared for her waking my mum up at such a time. However she relayed all of the news to them. I heard every word. She was charming and caring. She explained what had happened and that I was stable but still in A & E. She told them that she would ring again later and let them know how I was. I was eternally grateful.

As I became more aware of her presence I calmed down, reassured that I was not totally alone. Since there seemed to be little I could do I began to resign myself to my predicament. I decided I would take each minute on its merit and try not to think too far ahead. I drifted for a while, unable to sleep, not really listening to what was going on around me, and no particular thought in my head. My only highlight was the repeated return of the nurse who cared for me through the early hours of that day. I was to lay there for another six and a half hours. I found it degrading, tiring and concerning considering I had been diagnosed with dysentery. I couldn't believe I should be laying near other people and emitting my potentially dangerous and contaminated effluent. No one else seemed to be bothered however so I went with the flow. I could feel my eyelids becoming heavy and as it seemed to be the best way of shutting out my embarrassing predicament I let them close for a while.

I suddenly woke up. It was 4 am and my angel was next to me checking all of the usual monitors. "Hi, only me. Just checking you are ok. You ok if we leave this on? Your blood pressure is down again. How do you feel?" she asked. "Feel ill and tired; a bit confused" I replied. "It will be ok. You are in safe hands. Everything will be ok." I could have kissed her. Over the next three hours and until she went off shift I clung to her arrival like a limpet on a ship. I looked forward to seeing her, her smell, her touch and the sound of her voice. She brightened my spirits in a dreadfully dull place. I was very lucky to have been under her care. "Thank God for angels" I thought.

I drifted in and out of a very light sleep. Most of the time, I remained awake. The noise of people talking, the bleep of an odd machine and the passing trade was a mixture which defied much needed sleep, even in my condition. I started listening to individual conversations. The debate about the admission form was still ongoing. The form had changed in both structure and length. Certain parts needed filling in for this hospital and other parts for use in different hospitals. Parts of the form were so obscure that even the veterans of the department were clueless as to how to fill it in. It had clearly not been discussed before it turned up and it was evident no one had received any training relevant to it. I thought about all of the forms I had to fill in as a farmer. It seemed obscure that DEFRA could provide reams of instruction manuals to explain every fine point of detail on their forms. It usually took me a day to get through just reading the booklets about the forms. Then there was the vast array of administrators on telephones waiting to help anyone who struggled with interpretation. I couldn't believe that in an A&E department the NHS just created new administration without support. What if the form was filled in incorrectly? Might someone die? It seemed rather more urgent than whether wheat should be classified as OT1.

The nurse's conversations drifted back on to holidays and friends, as well as nights out and how much they enjoyed getting hammered on a Friday. How desperately ill Susan had been last week when she didn't get in until 3 in the morning and I was kind of pleased it was a Tuesday morning as their night life sounded reserved on a Monday night. They discussed husbands and boyfriends in intimate detail, anticipated holidays and shift changes with contrasting enthusiasm. Phones occasionally rang and interrupted their chit chat. Departments called each other. The pattern seemed to be ironing out communication or administration problems. It appeared that communiqués often drifted off message and needed reaffirming and that interdepartmental patient notes were misinterpreted by different people.

At about 4.45 am there was a bustle of activity as another elderly lady joined our ranks. "Abdominal pains. Low blood pressure, short of breath" a paramedic barked out. They laid her on a trolley. "That's it, lay her flat." "Oh Christ she's gone out. " Mild panic ensued. There was a rush of running and shouting and equipment being wheeled in. After a few minutes of concerned observation there was a happy declaration. "Breathing ok; obs ok. Nah, she's alright." She was wheeled in to some space to my left and a curtain pulled round. The nurses all returned to their station and normality ensued. Apart from a Doctor coming down to see to the lady a little later and an avid discussion about why she went out like a light when they layed her flat, not much else happened to her. I think she was still there when I eventually left later the next day. I had assumed that with such a crisis situation developing and her condition being so unstable that she would have received far more attention. I was pleased that I had shouted now. Maybe that's what you had to do.

A little later my curtain opened and my favourite nurse came in. "Ok we are taking you for an x ray. Are you ok to go now? " I nodded in the affirmative as the gift of speech had left me. She drew back the curtain and wheeled me out through the swing doors to the left of my curtain. Once through the doors it was a quick trip along the passage to the x ray department. "Ok I'm leaving you here for a while. They will be out to see you shortly and I will be back to pick you up. Ok?" More nodding. After a short wait the x ray doors opened and the radiologist walked around to the end of my trolley and without as much as a hello pushed me through the now closed doors with a clatter. I watched my IV drip bounce against the door and felt the canula pull on the back of my hand. She parked me in the middle of the room and proceeded to prepare her equipment. "Lean forward; hold your breath; lay flat; hold your breath; Keep still," she barked. As the radiologist took her photos it was clear that she had the bedside manner of a concentration camp guard. As soon as she had finished with me, again without a word, she backed me out of her doors and then left me with a picture or two at my feet staring up at the passageway ceiling. "Up yours too" I thought. But as I had been well brought up I managed "Thank you" but with no radiology department response. After a ten minute wait the angel returned and with her usual questions about my welfare wheeled me back from whence I came.

For the rest of those early hours of Tuesday the angel kept turning up to deal with my needs. I had never heard her voice entering the debates around the nurse's station. I wasn't sure if she was a sister or a staff nurse or any other sort of nurse. All I knew was that she had been exemplary in her approach to caring for me. When 7.00am arrived it was shift change. She popped in and said she was off home. "Someone will be in to see you soon. Hope you get on ok." And she was gone. It suddenly seemed a lonely place again.

Shift Change.

Despite having requested an update on my likely eventual location I remained in grumpy ignorance. My curtained off bay remained a sanctuary. A new member of staff, part of the day shift, poked her head around the curtain, looked at me, said "Hello" and then departed again leaving the curtain open by a couple of feet. I couldn't find the energy to call her back. I couldn't believe I was still in the A & E department some seven hours after my initial admission at the reception and particularly considering my diagnosis. On top of that I missed the Angel.

Finally a new nurse came in and offered a "Hello." She asked me some relevant questions about my admission which indicated a distinct lack of communication between shifts about ongoing patient care. I answered her in brief; aware as ever, of the repetitive nature of my answers. After doing my obs which seemed more stable and indicated an improving BP, she took away the commode. Unfortunately it didn't come back. I assumed she had more pressing issues and left it at that. After quarter of an hour it had still not returned and I was becoming anxious as although the length of time between episodes had increased there was still an ongoing requirement for the jolly piece of cardboard.

After a while I began to call out. I started with "Excuse me." After a few mild attempts at attracting polite attention I increased the request to a double "Excuse me, Excuse me" adding a couple of decibels and a slightly irritated tone. I could hear the nurses at the station as clear as a bell.

Surely they could hear me. I decided to change the message as pressure was starting to build. "Hello, help please!" didn't seem to make a great deal of difference. With an impending bullock like explosion about to exit my body it was clear I needed the reactions of trained athletes rather than shelf stackers at the local coop. "HEY, IS ANYONE THERE PLEASE?" I bellowed. My new nurse, who by the sound of it had to interrupt her story about a recent night out, was clearly less experienced and competent at the patient care part of her role. Maybe the day shift were the "B" team. As she came through the curtain she offered, "Yes?" in that slightly elongated vowel version which intimated a degree of annoyance at the interruption. "Sorry" I apologised "I need the commode." Realising my predicament she set off after it, returning in under a minute with everything I needed. "Now look, this time please don't mix everything up, ok?" Struggling to come to terms with exactly what I had done wrong I asked for clarification. "Melina in the cardboard, wipes on the top of the commode, no fluids. Understand?" It appeared that she wanted me to hold in my bladder. I suggested that maybe it would be appropriate if someone supplied me with a receptacle for bladder contents. And so some seven hours after admission I was given more bits of cardboard for all of my exhausted bodily emissions. I suddenly had enough bits of cardboard around me to analyse my own personal hour by hour carbon footprint. What I couldn't believe was that considering the dysentery issue and the fact that it is almost always contracted through direct contact I was expected to leave wipes lying around on top of a commode. It seemed to me to be an extremely unsanitary experience in a very high risk environment. When I considered the degree of risk assessments, COSHH assessments and general HSE paraphernalia I had to go through in my own day to day work on a farm I was exasperated at the lack of attention to detail there appeared to be in this hospital environment. I had heard all sorts of stories and read articles in the local press about the super bug problems this hospital had experienced over the last year. I was suddenly experiencing a concern about my exposure to them.

After a while the new shift nurse returned and changed my IV bag. The old IV had in its shrivelled and contracted state started to remind me of how I felt, so I was pleased to see its replacement swinging in healthy plump fashion above me. I didn't enjoy the saline in to the back of my hand as much however. The nurse needed to push the fluid through which unblocked my IV tube as it had crusted up.

I was becoming aware of a sense of emptiness. I hadn't eaten for 24 hours and I had lost a great deal of blood. My bowels, which were still bleeding, were cleared out. Even so, I had no appetite at all. I craved sleep above all else, but with the new shift activity and associated noise there was little opportunity for that. I began to listen to the bustle of a morning and realised it was pretty similar to the last seven hours. The nurses' station sounded like the night shift. It was a 'He said, she said; Ooh Egypt or Florida? Definitely going back though. Oh, did she?; what about that shift? No way I've already told 'em; I've done 32 hours this week already; That pods still bust Carol; John didn't come home till 10 last night; have you seen him on security, this morning, new guy, funny nose." So it went on in a perpetual stream of babble mixed with girly giggles and an occasional pacy double entendre. I didn't catch a word about Mrs Jones still lying somewhere to the east of me and clearly not making much noise. Ever since her demise of "going out like a light" she seemed to have shown little indication of life. I assumed someone had kept an eye on her. I didn't hear any discussion about patient care or about managing the department. A Paramedic team came in. By this point my curtain was pulled back far enough to observe them leaning on the nurse's station drinking cups of coffee. The discussions were all about how they felt and how hard their jobs were, how stupid Bill was and how useless the management was. It hadn't been a busy night by all accounts. One person had been collected by ambulance and then on reaching hospital had been picked up by relatives and driven home before they were admitted. A degree of confusion still existed as to what her exact condition was meant to have been. Occasionally one person asked another whether they had seen the BP kit and it appeared that they had just missed picking up a fatal car accident victim. They were beaten to it by another crew. Listening to the details about the victim was not high on my agenda.

The nurses talked over the paramedic crew, "Where are those new admission sheets? God how do you fill those in?" "What's happening about this pod? There are loads of blood samples here and loads of notes that need to go". I wondered how many of them were mine taken earlier that morning. "It still isn't working. What if you hit it? I gave it a smack last week and it started working. It's been dodgy for ages." The pod system, a pneumatic tube like delivery system which jets pods around the departments seemed to be inoperable. After a certain amount of tapping and poking followed by the inevitable expletives it was decided that someone needed to run the various samples and notes to the respective departments. How long some of these samples had been there was difficult to judge. I hoped hours more than days. "I suppose I will have to take these up to Haematology" one nurse declared, "I've nowt else to do for a bit". It captured the essence of the day shift admirably. What amazed me at the time was that there seemed an apparent lack of a maintenance department. I thought back to the state of the lavatory, the black tape on my trolley holding a rip in the cushion as well as the broken pod. It seemed there were too few running repairs being conducted which seemed strange considering how large an organisation this hospital clearly was. Like the hospital, I was also slowly dropping to bits and similarly didn't seem to have a maintenance crew to hand.

By 9.30 am I had started to believe that this was to be my final resting place. All of the stories that are written in the tabloids about patients being left in corridors for hours sprang to mind. I found it difficult to relate to how a hospital on a busy night found sufficient beds for incoming patients based on my experience. I questioned one of the nurses about my next move. They made a call to another department. It was clear from the phone call that there was still nothing available elsewhere on the wards. A nurse came back to my trolley and explained in an apologetic fashion that there seemed to be a hold up on the wards and that I would just have to wait. With no new developments, sub standard care, a feeling of exhaustion and the ever recurrent time spent hovering over a piece of cardboard, my spirit remained on edge.

It was encouraging news when fifteen minutes later and in stark contrast to my recent enquiry, the same nurse informed me that a porter would be with me shortly. I began to wonder exactly what the hospital used for a communication system, tin cans and string perhaps! It transpired that a room had suddenly come free and as a result I would be moved up to an isolation room. My initial feeling of good fortune and relief was tempered by mild disarray in my mind as to what "sudden" might have implied for the previous occupant. Nonetheless, since I had been suffering from the feeling of becoming an ever greater liability to the A & E department over the last few hours I was pleased to be on the move. Maybe my arrival at a new destination with a new set of nursing staff would deliver a fresh and enthusiastic caring regime. I made myself ready for the move. A nurse arrived to collect the various monitors from me. All that remained plugged in was my drip.

At 9.45 am a porter arrived to collect me. It was clear from the outset that despite his middle years and ownership of a perfectly fit body in working order, it would be a difficult if not impossible task to push me to the wards on his own. One of the nurses peeled off from talking about snorkelling and proceeded to help the porter transport me away from A & E. As I watched the strip lights pass above me like clouds in a summers sky on a breezy day it was clear that in fact the porter needed someone to talk to. "Bloody car wouldn't start this morning. Was late in. Didn't get ere till half past eight. Been chasing me tail ever since. Do you know I didn't get finished till 5.30 last night. It's not on." I felt like reaching up off my trolley grabbing him by the lapel and explaining that I was rather uninterested in the ramifications of what most would consider to be the irrelevant minutiae of his domestic affairs. I of course just kept watching the lights. Just as I calmed myself his able assistant piped up. "Oh I've had three crap days. We've had a lot of people through A & E. Had one die yesterday." "Oh, what of?" the porter interjected. "Don't know exactly. It's just hectic all of the time. I've still not got the drain sorted out at home. It's always dark when I get back. I think Brian has got the holiday booked. Very expensive. Sammy has got to go to have her driving lesson tonight so I shall nip off a bit earlier." The conversation was interrupted. "Jim are you there, over." The two way radio had spoken on the porter's belt. An air of importance entered his voice. "Yeah here. On way to ward with patient. Left A & E approx 5 minutes. ETA ward approx 3 minutes. Over" "Ok call in when you have dropped off." "Ok , out." It sounded like a jet fighter pilot communicating with the con tower, but with about one hundredth of the intelligence. "I reckon one came in last night from a car crash dead." Piped up the nurse, "Pleased I wasn't on nights. " And so it rumbled on. To me it all seemed surreal. Each sentence and each pace up the corridor felt like I was being taken further and further away from reality and deeper and deeper in to the bowels of the institution. Somewhere I guessed there was an element of truth in the stories but a combination of Chinese whispers and embellishment of the story for the benefit of the teller had probably altered the reality over the course of time. I wondered how much the mindset of the staff, the environment they worked in and the lack of vision and motivation provided by the management affected their day to day lives. It occurred to me that this chatter was their way of coping with the imperfect environment they lived in every day. I was just a visitor. Even so as a patient it wasn't easy listening and it wasn't doing my state of mind any good at all. I couldn't escape it unless I jumped off the trolley. I wondered whether they would notice.

Isolation.

After a change of floors via a lift and a brief few yards along a further corridor we arrived at an admissions ward. "Where do you want him?" I felt like a piece of meat being transported along the shop floor at Smithfield Market. I have to say having been to Smithfield market there seemed to be more useful people about generally in the early hours than had been evident in A&E. Needless to say, I smelt far worse than a piece of well hung meat. I was tired, anxious and very uncertain about my immediate future. They pushed me into a room where I appeared to have sole occupancy. It had walls and a window. This marked a significant improvement to the floor space in A & E. I felt like this was perhaps an end to my indignity. The window was partly open and an icy breeze crept around the room. The paint on the walls was tired and in places it was flaked away to expose some plasterwork requiring repair. It was basically furnished with a bed, two plastic chairs and a medical style cabinet next to the bed. A table was also parked nearby. The bed was unmade and the stained pillows were without their cases. The curtains that were hung in the window occasionally moved in the breeze and showed an ugly mark on one side. With an, "on three" they lifted me from my trolley to the unmade bed. Without so much as a 'goodbye' both the porter and the nurse headed out of the room. I could just hear the porter reporting in to mission control. "One dropped off at admissions, waiting for instructions." I felt very alone. I thought about who had been in here before me.

I lay on the bed looking out at the grey horizon which occupied my view through the window. The sky reflected my mood. The nurse's station was just across the corridor from the isolation room and through the open door I could hear a familiar conversation. It was louder than it had been on A & E, and it followed a similar vein. It was bolstered by a wider selection of people which included doctors, cleaners and various other visiting medical staff. I listened intently as the conversations competed with each other for air space. The subjects were, as ever, majoring on anything other than the medical profession. Holidays, time off work, people, families, television and nights out were under discussion. Very occasionally someone made a relevant medical contribution such as, 'where is that list?' or 'what are we doing about that bed?' But even then other conversations about their social lives competed constantly. The sound intruded into my space and took away the bit of privacy I had tried to enjoy. I didn't want to have to listen to other people's conversations. All I wanted was to be able to draw confidence from the sound of an efficient department with a dedicated team sounding like they were on top of their job. As I continued to be bombarded by their chatter I found myself already questioning their ability and their dedication.

After being left in the room for about ten minutes a male staff nurse came in and introduced himself as Bill. "I'm going to be looking after you, ok?" He explained about the new technology I now had on offer. Above my head in its retainer there was a hand held device which if I pressed the picture of a nurse, one would arrive. That would be novel after my recent experience in A & E. Unfortunately the light switch didn't work and the other buttons which were for radio were obsolete too, so the only part that worked was the nurse button. I hoped he was right. To my right was a television which had an IT screen and telephone attached to it. After a 5 minute presentation from Bill I was led to understand that if I paid some money in to the machine down the corridor I would be able to receive a credit card which I could plug in to the TV. Once I had then registered via the telephone with the necessary authorities I would be allowed to watch the TV for a set number of hours until my money ran out. I thanked him and explained that I wasn't that bothered but before much longer I would need facilities of the cardboard kind. In my mind I just hoped that they didn't want me to pay for the trees that would need to be cut down or expect me to carbon offset their use as well.

After a short while he returned with a commode and an armful of differently shaped bits of cardboard. He left me to it, but as he left he failed to close the door which remained wide open. I wondered whether I should try out the nurse's button to see whether 'door shutting' fell in to their domain. By the time I had reached up for the handset I was almost out of bed anyway. I climbed off the unmade bed. The drip tube was stretched as far as it would allow. I just managed to make the door with my left hand and swung it shut without pulling the drip out of my hand. Oddly no one at the nurse's station noticed my contortions. After arranging the various cardboard components I managed to relieve myself with a modicum of dignity. It was clear from the result of my contortions that the bleed was subsiding. Once I had managed to climb back on to bed I called for a nurse. Even if door shutting wasn't one of their regular activities I was convinced commode services certainly was! The technology seemed to be working. It was certainly a vast improvement to shouting. Bill arrived, and before I had time to finish explaining about there being a need for emptying, he immediately set off with the contents. Rather him than me.

Within a few minutes a new doctor, Doc 3 turned up. I was beginning to think that at medical school, lesson number one must be, 'Ask the patient the following questions in this particular order' as he immediately went through the same 20 questions both Doc 1 and 2 had been through. It seemed that they were very good at asking questions but very under par at recording the answers. I wondered whether they listened to the answers. 'Charles Davey?' "No, Edward" "Says Charles here" "Yes, just because its there as a first name doesn't necessarily mean I use it" I thought, but instead explained that I preferred Edward. "D.O.B. ?, When did your symptoms begin? What are your symptoms? Have you taken any drugs, alcohol, are you allergic" and so it went on and on. Once he had finished wasting his and my time I asked him whether anyone knew more details about my condition and diagnosis. I wondered whether the X rays had shown anything. "We think you have an infection, probably dysentery. You will need to stay in isolation. At this stage we cannot say any more. One of the consultants will be up to see you later. "With that and a handshake, which really seemed an inappropriate thing to do to a patient with dysentery, he was gone. He of course left the door wide open. I was beginning to wonder what isolation actually meant.

Apart from a cat nap in A & E I had not managed sleep since 6.00am the previous day. In reality I had been through 30 hours without sleep and experienced a stressful series of events. I guessed I resembled a dishevelled tramp. I was gaunt, pale and unshaven. Surely even a student nurse was taught that rest was integral to cure. I wondered what qualifications this department had in patient care as the tittle tattle at the nurse's desk was loud enough to wake the dead. If that wasn't enough the temperature in the room resembled a morgue. I lay with one thin hospital blanket pulled over me on the still unmade bed. The window was out of range of my IV drip and I couldn't summon the energy to requisition someone to close it. The draught had its upside as the fresh air did at least improve the smell of the place. Unable to sleep and still suffering from regular cardboard filling moments I existed through the remainder of the morning. My mind drifted along with the day. I tried not to dwell on what had gone on and began to think about what may be ahead. I wondered whether anyone would be coming to see me today. I gathered visiting started at 2pm. I hoped desperately that someone would arrive and sort out my care.

In one moment of inspiration two nurses came in and proceeded to make the bed around me. Pillow cases, bed sheets and an extra larger pillow enabling me to sit up comfortably made my residence more comfortable and the bed more hospitable. It was definitely an improvement. They checked my obs. It was the first time since I had arrived in the isolation room that anyone had done anything particularly medical. BP was still a bit low, but everything else seemed ok. Not long afterwards another doctor came in, Doc 4. He looked at a few notes that had started to appear on my clip board. A stool chart and BP chart were forming for analyses. He smiled and walked out without introducing himself. I wasn't alone for long. With a flurry of other medical staff surrounding him, like gnats around your head on a summer's evening, in came a consultant. Con 1 had arrived. I suddenly realised that the frenetic preceding activity was more for his benefit than mine. He might not have liked one of his patients lying under a dirty blanket on an unmade bed on his shift.

His no nonsense persona reeked of authority and whilst I was slightly intimidated, I was also reassured that Con 1 might have the answers I was looking for. "Hello Mr

Davey". He introduced himself. "Now I believe you came in through casualty last night, is that correct?" "Yes." I then received the now ad verbatim 20 question routine. I felt like asking what the pens in their top pockets were for. Maybe if someone wrote down the answers you could all have them at the same time? "We are not really sure what's going on at this stage. Lost a lot of blood? " "Yes," I mumbled. "Ok. We will be keeping you in. We need to observe you and probably do some tests. Are you in pain?" "No," I answered. "Tell me about what happened". I started at the beginning of when I fell ill. "No, more about what it looks like" "Dark red" "How regular?" I explained as best I could. I couldn't quite understand why I had bothered crouching over bits of cardboard for the last 12 hours if they didn't bother keeping samples or at least write down their observations so that Con 1 or his ilk could be conveyed the details. Eventually after a Gestapo style questioning session which contained a continuing reference to dysentery he declared that he would see me later. He turned sharply, nearly walking into one of his minions scribbling on a clip board behind him, stopped, shuffled to the left and before I could summon the energy to ask whether I might live or die, he left the room with his wake of followers. My opinion of him dropped a couple of notches. He had just been about as helpful as a chocolate fire guard.

Within a few minutes a new lady wearing a blue overall poked her head through the door. "Cup of tea, love? Biscuit ?" I was momentarily in shock. Surely I shouldn't be drinking tea. "Sorry I replied I'm not sure whether I am allowed anything to drink. Perhaps you should check" She duly set off to ask the pertinent questions. After a matter of seconds she popped her head through the door, "Good job you're on the ball. Sorry not allowed it. Bye for now." I wondered what the sign on the door was for, the one which I hoped had my name on it with 'nil by mouth' below it.

By the time everyone had finished poking their heads through the door it was clear I needed to affect the balancing act between my IV bag and the door to enable some privacy to conduct my usual disgraceful habit. At full stretch I reached the door with my foot and pushed it closed to achieve some privacy. I still just couldn't be bothered to ask a nurse to close the door for me.

As 2pm grew ever nearer, the bouts of blood loss and Melina became ever less frequent. I had more time to think about the bigger picture issues. I began to realise that there would be a number of people who were expecting me to arrive at certain destinations soon and would need to be informed of my predicament. I decided I had better get the phone working and proceeded to deal with the administration powers that be, using my debit card to establish my financial credibility. Once I had a lifeline I proceeded to call the various people concerned. I had an important assessment day with the NFU which I was clearly not going to make in a few days time. When I called them to apologise they were very sympathetic and concerned. I felt relieved to find out that so far my illness hadn't prevented that particular opportunity. My Nuffield was slightly more difficult. I didn't want to just make a call to the director and declare my lack of availability. Certain members of the organisation knew as a result of various interviews and discussions the degree of importance I had placed upon it. My referees, support network and advisors were all too aware of how much a moment in time this era had become. I called Martin, a long time friend, previous Nuffield scholar and my mock interviewer. He was shocked and disappointed to hear about my quandary. His initial reaction about my care was swiftly followed by a request for a prognosis and a timescale in order to try and achieve some degree of compromise at the Nuffield end. I was unfortunately unable to tell him anything. I appealed to his generosity to call and make my apologies to the interview panel and the director. I also asked him to investigate my options at this stage assuming a recovery hypothesis was put forward. As always his natural humour and optimistic outlook as well as his reassurances that my best interests would be served improved my spirits. He was taken aback that this had happened and disappointed that I wasn't going to be allowed my opportunity. I had a lump in the throat when I put the phone down.

I called my Mum. After the initial few minutes and the 'Motherly' 20 questions, as opposed to the usual 'Medical' 20 questions, she realised I wasn't going to die on the spot. She was full of concern and I could hear from her voice that she was understandably worried about me. I asked her to call Chrissie and let her know I wouldn't be making London. Evidently the jungle drums had been beating through most of the morning as everyone had already been told I was in hospital. I needed to make sure cover was in place to look after Bramble. The poor old dog wasn't a lot better than me to be fair and would need some nurturing. Mum assured me that she would make sure Bramble went to stay with Sandra and that she would be fine. Mum promised to be in sometime during the afternoon and after various reassuring maternal noises I managed to get off the phone. I was also meant to be travelling up to the Borders in about a week's time with my pals for a long weekend in to the Lammermuir hills. I reckoned that if I was very lucky I might be fit for the trip but since there was a lot of cost attached I needed to make sure I was covered in the eventuality of not making it. When I called the 'Captain' it was clear that my imminent no show was of great concern. The posse would miss me and I was not to worry about the finances. Even so it was a real wrench to even consider not making it as it was the highlight of the year going up there with my friends. After these various calls which brought reality back in to my life,

I no longer felt alone. Even so the calls had unfortunately reemphasised all of the opportunities I had so been looking forward to. That felt a bit grim.

2pm ticked by. My day became a mixture of cardboard gymnastics, visits from Bill, the one man 'UXB' disposal team, glances out of the window, the insipid stories of local nightlife and an occasional nurse administering to my vital signs. I received a further visit from another overall clad lady offering me tea and as before I sent her graciously on her way. I then received a visit from a nurse bearing a jug of water and a plastic cup. "You can sip some water, ok?" "Thanks "I said. "Terrific" I thought. I wondered why they bothered with the signs on the door if they never changed them or read them. Should I or should I not drink?

As the afternoon wore on I became evermore expectant of my visitors arrival. I was very pleased to see Mum and Dad when they arrived. I guessed I looked ill by the concern in their faces. Nonetheless their familiar faces were a great tonic and they were genuinely relieved to see me in one piece. They had clearly been very concerned about me. I felt better having them there and with a few day to day essentials like the newspaper, a toothbrush and some fresh underwear near to hand. It seemed strange that considering I was in isolation they were allowed to be with me, touch me and kiss me. I was sure there should be some sort of horrible gown and glove set up you had to wear on these occasions. Even so I was pleased that they didn't have to undergo it as it was far more humane without. After lots of reassurances that I was unlikely to slip my mortal coil and plenty of stories about my experiences and the concerns I had about the hospital so far, Mum set to work on sorting out my care. She wandered outside to the nurse's station and made noises about a possible transfer to a private department or whether since the hospital was on our private medical insurance list whether it would be possible to see a consultant for a private consultation. She was told that she would have to speak to a consultant directly. Armed with this information she declared to me that on her return she would try to lobby for some information about what was likely to happen to me. She also promised more homely possessions. I missed them almost immediately upon their departure. For a moment there seemed a small chance of regaining a bit of control in to both my life and my health management with their support. My room was quiet and lonely in their absence.

Unannounced, a new nurse came in and declared that I would be 'nil by mouth' for the foreseeable future. The jug of water was instantly dispatched and I began to wonder whether they knew what they were doing. She returned to do my obs and proceeded to conduct another series of blood samples. I was wondering whether there was any blood left in my legs, never mind my arms.

After an hour or so of staring out of the window, contemplating burning some of my credit on the TV, or catching up with the hot gossip in the local rag which Mum had delivered earlier I was interrupted by Doc 5. He didn't spend long with me. After asking the obligatory 20 questions he got down to business. The blood tests had indicated that my haemoglobin levels had dropped significantly and my blood pressure was still a little bit off although oxygen levels were apparently normal. My haemoglobin level was down to 8 and in order to bring it back to its normal level of 13, I would need a blood transfusion. Haemoglobin is the iron-containing oxygen-transport metalloprotein in the red blood cells of the blood. He informed me that the transfusion would take place later tonight once they had crossed checked bloods and they had obtained the blood from haematology. I was advised that there was nothing to worry about and that the blood transfusion would correct the problem. He asked me whether there were any questions. Since I had little idea of what was involved or what he had just talked about and as I was feeling pretty tired I neglected to answer with any competent questioning. In hindsight and knowing what I know now I wish I had asked about the risks including reactions and infections of which there are several. I still find it rather strange that they don't explain the risks rather than ask the patient. Hepatitis is a pretty big thing and whilst low risk in this day and age, I felt worthy of comment once it later registered with me what was happening.

At about 6pm Mum returned with a number of additional essentials including a book to read. She unfortunately hadn't managed to make it to my place so the real luxury items of bed clothes and a razor remained something to look forward to. Once I explained the intended course of action and what was likely to happen to me she suggested that at least it would mean I would be staying in my isolation room which was a bonus. Still concerned for my welfare it was fortunate that Con I happened to walk past the door and so Mum set off to collar him in an attempt to find out whether any private treatment may be available. Despite her best attempts she returned perplexed and somewhat concerned. "He just put me off from getting anywhere," she explained. "He said that you have to stay under him and under the NHS as it is too risky to take you to the Private hospital since all of the resuscitation equipment is here. He said that was because you were having a blood transfusion tonight. " I obviously looked quizzically at her as she added, "Well, I don't know. Do you think we should ask someone else? I would have thought the private hospital would have resuscitation equipment too. These places are not always straightforward. You know when your Father was ill we had to work really hard to get to the bottom of things. No one seemed to really know what the matter was and there was a real lack of interest. If it hadn't been for Chris highlighting that it might be linked with the endocrine system we wouldn't have found it. Even when we went back we had to push for them to consider whether it could be that. It really is a case of 'He who shouts loudest'. If we hadn't made a lot of noise we would never have been down the right path. It's terrible really. You will just have to push Ed when you get the chance." Before I could answer she had already decided that she would spend some more time investigating the issues. It all seemed rather strange to me. I couldn't believe that a private hospital couldn't manage a patient in my condition and that considering how long I had already been in, no one was prepared to analyse my medical history in detail or learn more about my symptoms. It just didn't make sense. As Mum left she promised to make a few calls when she got home to various friends who may be able to answer some of our questions as to why it wasn't possible to be seen privately or at least get another opinion on my condition. I missed her once she was gone.

As I lay alone in my room I felt incredibly isolated. I was in danger of feeling sorry for myself when something occurred to me. I probably wasn't dying. I was neither old nor very young and so at far less risk than either. There were far worse situations to be in and within this very hospital I knew there would be very many people far more sick than myself. There may even be someone dying. I wasn't in ITU, or a high dependency unit. Whatever my prognosis was, it was clear that the general opinion indicated a stable case despite all of my recent activity which suggested otherwise. If it was more serious I would have been despatched to intensive care by now. That is of course assuming that there was room, they had such a unit and there were any staff on it. It was a sobering thought that there were some very sick people somewhere in the hospital and one which I had so far spent little time considering. I knew how scared I had been and reflected what it must be like if you were old and dependent or young and frightened and either severely injured or desperately ill. I felt both sad and embarrassed at the same time. Moreover I was immediately full of concern about anyone in such a situation who may have experienced the same level of care as me. One assumes that the level of care in such a unit would be of the highest order. Having seen the A&E department I was less convinced of who might be in charge of ITU or HDU. It galvanised me into trying to get better rather than deteriorating, as the prospect of falling into the hands of some fish and chip eating hooligans in ITU was extremely concerning. I didn't fancy them opening me up using plastic knives and forks they just had handy. As I drifted into a restless few minutes of sleep I said a little prayer for anyone who needed it.

My phone rang. It was mum. She had been busy behind the scenes fact finding. It was apparent that Con 1 was a cardiologist. She explained that there was another consultant in the hospital who was an eminent local gastroenterologist. She was going to make some more calls to determine whether it was possible for me to be seen by him. Even to a layman it was apparent that there was little wrong with my heart. It had in everyone else's opinion done a very good job of coping, even without its usual supply of the red stuff. She had also been told that Con 1 was a difficult man to deal with. He was very anti private treatment and tended to have a large say in hospital policy. It appeared he was a man that was feared on the wards rather than loved, by both nurses and consultants alike. It had been mentioned that he liked to be in control and was very forceful in his approach. Whilst slightly concerned that I might be under a complete bastard, I was now in the full knowledge that there was an in depth research project underway behind the scenes in support of my cause. Or at least I hoped so. I rested easier than I had for a while. I realised it was ages since I had used anything of a cardboard nature. Things were on the up!

Archangel.

As the evening developed I occasionally dropped off to sleep. Usually the noise from the corridor only allowed a few minutes at a time. As I awoke on one occasion, an archangel arrived by my bed. I suppose any man is going to be slightly biased when a very pretty nurse is looking after him. Whilst I noticed her looks, it wasn't that alone which made me remember her. She was genuinely interested in me and asked questions about how I felt and whether there was anything I needed. She sorted out the icy blast from my window and made sure my bed was straight. She always pulled the door to and tried to make sure I remained undisturbed. There were immediate similarities to the angel who had cared for me in A & E. If I had realised I would only benefit from her care for that one night I would have spent more time pressing my nurse's button. When she arrived at my bedside it was always with a smile and with caring concern. When she checked my vital signs and tested my blood pressure and temperature it was with the most professional demeanour. When she talked to me it was always with an enquiring respect and a sympathetic manner. I asked her whether the intended blood transfusion was still going ahead. It was clear that she knew little about it but disappeared off and within no time at all returned to inform me that it would be, and that she would administer it. Suddenly there was joy in being ill. As the evening wore on she told me about her two children, one of nearly 4 and another only 8 months old. She had only returned to work from maternity leave in November and she still missed the family. She talked about her husband back at home looking after the kids. In all of her short stories she humanised my dull, cold and uninviting isolation room. As I listened I became increasingly jealous of her lucky husband. It would be a joy to have this archangel walking through your door at the end of a shift. She changed my IV and after a while came back with a pump and a drip stand to accommodate my blood. "Ok do you understand what we are going to do?" I replied in the affirmative but with little enthusiasm as I was now without proper sleep for about 40 hours and I still felt very drained and ill. I raised enough energy to ask whether they could check it was the right blood. "How do you mean the right blood?" "I don't want any of that blood which either makes you incapable of reversing a car or talking endlessly to your mother on the phone on a Sunday morning!" "You what?" she asked. I explained to her, "None of that blood which sends you shoe shopping for hours, gives you headaches and makes you remember every bodies birthdays." I looked at her completely expressionless face which indicated that she thought I was going insane. "You know, female blood!" As it slowly dawned on her, a smile crept across her face and she kindly laughed. "I can see we are going to have trouble with you." She turned and left the isolation room. I could hear her as she reached the nurse's station and retold the story to her colleagues. I could hear a ripple of laughter and I hoped it put me in a better light with them. As the clock struck 10 she hooked up the transfusion and after reassuring me that it was definitely 'male blood' and it only ever thought about one thing, she explained more seriously that it had been treated and was safe. She started regulating it in to my body through the pump. An adult has between 7 and 9 pints of blood in the body. I received 2 pints to help my system catch up and improve my haemoglobin level. It would take all night for the 2 pints. The pump regulated it into my body in a series of measured pulses with an associated sleep depriving bleep with each pulse. I could feel the new blood seeping into my veins and I wondered whether any change would be apparent as a result of my new genetics. I began to wonder who had donated it and how delighted I was that someone had. At the same time I was receiving IV fluid in to the other arm. During the night I received a further 4 units of IV fluid in addition to the 2 units of blood. My archangel came and changed each one. Sometimes I would be asleep and she would gently wake me with the lightest touch on my arm. "It's ok. It's only me. I'm just changing a bag. You ok?" Funnily enough I was.

Confusion reigned at about 1.00 am as a new male nurse I hadn't met before appeared at my bedside. I didn't know who he was. He immediately started fiddling with my pump and drips. I asked him what was happening. He explained that I was going to be moved out of my room. I was shocked. It was 1.00 am, I was mid transfusion with about a quarter of my first unit left to drip into my body. I was really tired. I explained that I had so far been diagnosed with dysentery and believed I needed to remain in isolation. Where was my favourite nurse? He left the room explaining that he would confirm things once he had enquired about my surprising reservations.

He didn't return. My first thoughts were that he had been mistaken. I even wondered whether he was a nurse at all. However the archangel came back and when I asked her she confirmed that I would be moved onto a ward. I again showed some distress. She went off to make a call and upon her return advised me that it now appeared that they didn't believe it be dysentery. I wasn't sure whether I was confused, relieved or more concerned about what it might be if it wasn't dysentery. She could see my unease. "Don't worry. Try to rest. It would be good if you could get some sleep." Whilst I agreed with her whole heartedly there was little chance for sleep other than cat naps. Apart from the pump bleeping at me every few seconds, there was nearly as much noise from the corridor at night as in the day. I fell into a short troubled sleep for perhaps 15 or 20 minutes until I was disturbed again by the male nurse that had arrived earlier. Without a word he began to collect up my belongings and place them in to a bag which he put behind my head on the bed. After checking my IV and transfusion and somehow wheeling both my pumps and bed at the same time he headed for the door. As he pushed me in to the brightly lit corridor he carelessly hooked one of the pumps around the door knob and yet proceeded to cart me further in to the corridor. I was aware of the problem almost immediately as I spotted the pump falling behind. I lifted up my arm which was attached to the pump and threw it backwards over my head. Unbelievably the male nurse seemed to be in some sort of a trance. My arm shot further back towards the room as he continued to push me out of it. As I began to feel the canula tighten on the back of my hand I lifted myself up to create more slack and cried out, "Hey, look out." He immediately came to a halt as he realised what he had done. "Oops, sorry mate" he exclaimed. 'Mate' wasn't the word I had in mind. 'Cretin', 'Idiot' and 'Mindless pillock' fitted the bill. He fumbled about until he had control over everything again, rearranged the pump and then continued to wheel me down the corridor. He turned left in to the first entrance we came to. It was dark. With a growing sense of foreboding, I was wheeled in to the ward. I immediately spotted an elderly lady to my left. My heart sank. Not only was I going to be subjected to the humiliation of performing in public again but I was going to be expected to do it in front of the Women's Institute as well. I prayed for an immediate miracle cure and a total cessation of all activity of a digestive nature within my body.

It was either that or a teleport transport to a completely different planet. Once I was half way down the ward the 'mindless pillock' pushing my trolley backed me into the central bay without contact or any further accidents. I quickly took stock of my immediate environment. I had someone behind a drawn curtain to my right, no one to my left and a large man moaning and groaning in a bed across the corridor.

My insecurities and concerns were allayed to a degree by the arrival of archangel. "You ok?" she whispered. I wanted to desperately say 'No' and ask her whether she would either take me back to the isolation room or if at all possible home with her at the end of the shift. I nodded instead. She leant over and re arranged all of my tubes and connections. She smelt fantastic, clean and antiseptic yet feminine and sweet, all at the same time. She checked my blood pressure and temperature. Once she was convinced I was settled in she left me to my new surroundings.

The first thing you noticed was the noise. Across the way a large man was making the sort of sound that you imagined could be his last breath. Each time he went for air it sounded like he was sucking it through tracing paper and a comb. There was a horrible crackling noise towards the end of his intake which sounded like fluid in his lungs. His terrible reverberating rasp reflected the battle he was having holding on to life as he fought for fresh air. As the air exited his body it did so amongst a range of guttural sounds and mixed up commentary. His body never lay still and he constantly moved his legs about the bed, more often than not throwing them outside the parameters of his trolley, one side and then to the other. To his right the elderly woman I had first noticed on entering the ward murmured intermittently about her cat. To my right I could hear a persistent nasal snore which may have been male or female interrupted by occasional coughing. Along with the bleep of my pump there was sufficient noise to make sleep impossible. I wondered how the rest of the ward had managed it.

I couldn't believe that in this day and age patient privacy was still beyond the NHS as a concept. I suspected that even in Florence Nightingale's day there would have been a modicum of human dignity left to men and women when they were at their most vulnerable. Even if I hadn't been suffering from my embarrassing condition I would have felt quite concerned about my sudden lack of privacy. For some of the elderly patients who lay in the beds around me it must have been even worse. Since the majority of the patients within the NHS are elderly I couldn't understand why a mixed ward still existed. The impact upon an elderly patient's dignity, privacy and respect must be enormous. It wasn't exactly in the interests of the health service to affect people's psyche in such a negative way. Surely you wanted relaxed, happy and confident recovery. A patient with angst, concern and embarrassment would never achieve a state of mind that aided their recuperation. Two thirds of those in hospitals are over 65 years of age. Three quarters of them come in as an emergency. As a result, like me, they would have no choice about their care and would have to accept that which was administered to them. I tried to imagine what they felt like after two days on a mixed ward after being admitted through A & E. Bloody scared and very embarrassed!

As I couldn't sleep and because there was so much going on I peered in to the gloom across the way. The large man seemed to be in a very gritty struggle for his life. His noisy breathing was interrupted with grunts of 'out,out,out,' as he pushed his irritated legs beyond the confines of his covers and the bed. At times he nearly fell out of the bed and at one point he had achieved a 180 degree turn with his head out one side and his legs out of the other. As he started to fall he somehow forced himself back in to the bed, seemingly still asleep. I couldn't make out whether he was in some sort of coma or just suffering from a sleep disorder. Once in a while a nurse came in to see him. She would lay his legs back under the covers and straighten him up. "Now, Gordon, be a good lad and keep them legs in. Come on, now be good." Gordon was apparently oblivious to the request as no sooner had she left the ward than the legs would be free of their covers and splayed either east or west. Sometimes the breathing noise which emitted from his ailing body filled the entire room. It was a fearful noise. There was no escape from it. It was clear that Gordon was very ill. I was distressed by his condition and wished him a speedy recovery for not only his, but my own well being. I wondered why he wasn't in an isolation room himself. As the same nurse repeatedly attended him throughout the night it became clear that her patience and concern were equivalent to my archangels. Eventually when it became evident that Gordon was never going to comply with her requests, the nurse sat in the chair at his bedside. Every five to ten minutes when he shuffled or threw out his legs she would contain him, allay his concerns and calm him back in to a restful state. She eventually remained with him for about four hours never leaving his side.

Whilst I was shocked at being on a mixed ward, still unsure about my own diagnosis, incredibly tired, confused about so many events and unconvinced about a large degree of the care I had experienced thus far, I was truly impressed by this nurse's compassion and dedication. Her actions in combination with what I had learnt about my archangel's infinite nursing skills that night, made me realise that a dichotomy existed between the good and the bad within the NHS. Some people in the organisation were clearly very good at what they did and some were downright incompetent. There seemed to be a general lack of good management throughout the departments I had so far experienced. I had noticed considerable under spend on basic resources. The hospital was a dire environment to work in with a depressing environment, unhappiness and illness saturating your state of mind. As a patient, an awareness of death hung about like an occasional bad dream. The communication systems seemed old fashioned and inept at times. There was no consistency within the deployment of systems and approaches and there seemed little regard for taking responsibility outside one's department. As I lay there I began to feel as though the whole purpose for the design of the NHS had at some stage been forgotten and then lost. Patient care and healing should be the focus of the organisation. Yet the NHS seemed wrapped up in a day to day muddle which had been culturally invented at almost every level within the hospital and the service. In all there seemed to be no clear vision as to what everyone was meant to be achieving. I began to think about all of the different people who took a role in leadership within the NHS. Politicians, trust boards and managers all sprang to mind. Whilst I could see fault at the coalface too, such as the male nurse who tried to bring an early halt to my blood transfusion, it was clear that on the whole the staff were trying hard with the resources they had on offer. It was also clear that a great deal of the behaviour I had witnessed in the last day and a half was cultural and established as a result of the policies the organisation was run by.

As I considered all of these thoughts, I realised how lucky I was to be watched over by an Archangel.

Terror and Toyboys.

As Gordon continued to perform some crazy dance routine with his attendant nurse, a new member of our fraternity was wheeled in to my immediate left. It was only too obvious that she was feeling very ill. Her constant moans of discomfort crammed the room with suffering. Once the nurses who attended her had finished parking her trolley they asked whether she needed anything. "A bowl, I'm going to be sick again" she gurgled. She was right. Before the nurse managed to reach her, the splatter of the contents of her stomach hitting the ward floor subdued even Gordon's grumbling clatter. Once they had cleaned her up and whilst they were still in attendance she started to cry. Her soft intermittent sobs stole the last piece of happiness out of the room. I was within an arm's reach of her with only a curtain between our bays. Each damp sob increased my compassion. I wished I was able to perform some miracle to ease her discomfort.

Within a few minutes a doctor arrived. I felt a sense of relief in the knowledge that she would be cared for. I couldn't see him other than his ankles and shoes beneath the dividing curtain. It was 3 am. "Name?" he started with, and then proceeded to follow up with the usual 20 questions I had become used to. Once he had established her name, address, age and general details which I would have thought would have been available on an admissions sheet somewhere, he asked about her health. "How do you feel?" She felt disorientated, sick, scared and very unsure of her whereabouts. He began to ask specific questions about her health. It became evident that she was on medication and that she suffered from a degree of mental illness. She wasn't really sure how she had managed to get in to the hospital. It certainly wasn't her local hospital as that was some 15 mile south. He started to ask her more and more questions about her prescriptions and how many drugs she had taken and when she last took them. She answered his questions declaring that she hadn't taken anything that she shouldn't and that everything had been taken recently as per prescription. It was clear that he didn't believe her. He reaffirmed his questions. Occasionally she gave an inconsistent answer. I noticed that her voice had changed. There was a hint of fear. The Doctor was ramping up the questions, often repeating them and his approach was starting to upset the girl. He had raised his voice a little and there was a lack of patience or care within his tone. The more questions he asked, the more confused she became and so more and more upset. At one point the doctor exclaimed in a firm and somewhat melodramatic fashion. "Look, if you don't tell me what you have really done, you might die." At this her intermittent sobs became a constant flow of tears. Within a few seconds her misery was increased as she vomited in to what presumably was a bit of cardboard. "Did you realise that you were vomiting up some blood?" asked the doctor. The woman seemed beyond replying. A nurse quickly attended and removed the mess that had been created. She changed a sheet and then spent a few minutes cleaning her up again.

Whilst I could understand the doctor's frustration I was very surprised at the lack of care or respect this woman received. It was almost as though she was an inconvenience to everyone and that the doctor just wanted to force the information out of her so that he could tick her off a list and hand her on to someone else. He set off again with another series of questions. These were aimed at her recent health and whether she had attended any other medical facilities. She could hardly speak. Her unhappiness clearly consumed her. She tried to answer his questions. Sometimes she only managed half a sentence, before resuming into a pitiful heart rending sob. He didn't let up. I felt like I was entering a moral maze. Should I speak up on her behalf? ; Was it any of my business? ; Did I understand what was going on? I remained silent and very uncomfortable. His persistent badgering began to yield results as she forced herself to answer his questions. It was clear that over the last year she had been in to hospital, though not this one, on two separate occasions suffering from similar symptoms. No one had managed to discover anything and each time it had cleared up. There were a series of drugs which had been prescribed to her over time. It seemed they were relevant to stabilising her mental condition and anxieties. Some she continued to take, others had been abandoned on her GP's authority. The doctor armed with a degree of information set off, I suspected to discuss what he had learned with someone else. The crying returned as did the vomiting. He left her in a terrible state. I couldn't ever see him becoming a counsellor.

After about twenty minutes he returned with another doctor. It immediately set off a new series of weeping. They asked alternate questions in an almost 'good cop', 'bad cop' routine. The original doctor remained stand-offish and unsympathetic firing questions at her about why she had been admitted tonight and who had brought her? It was clear that she was meant to be seeing a specialist in a few days time at another hospital. She seemed bewildered and frightened. As the terror of the situation became more and more real for her, the sorrowful nerve racking experience started to impact upon her thought process. "I want to go home. Please let me go home. Leave me alone. Please, I just want to go home." I remembered how I had felt when I was sat back in the A & E waiting room and completely sympathised with her.

The doctors realised that they had squeezed as much out of her as they could and that their competence in appeasing a woman in distress was limited. They left the ward and their disturbed mess in the more capable hands of the nurses. Two nurses moved in to soothe her. Each talked quietly and reassuringly. For almost another 15 minutes the woman repeatedly pleaded to be allowed home. All the nurses could do was promise to arrange it. They took her husband's details and telephone number and promised to speak to him to arrange her collection. I somehow didn't believe them.

Once she had been left alone she cried the remainder of the night in to her pillow. I lay there consumed with disbelief at the inhumanity of the situation. It was 5.30 am. I had failed to sleep. Apart from the reassurance I received each time my archangel changed my fluid bags or checked my observations I was aghast at my recent experience of an admissions ward. I found the lack of respect shown to the poor woman almost incomprehensible. There seemed to be no consistency in the quality of care as it was dependent upon an individual's ability. It seemed madness to terrorise an individual particularly when her mental well being was itself in question. The common denominator seemed to be that the nurses carried the only beneficial values and principles towards patient care within the entire organisation.

As she settled down I began to fall asleep as the peace and quiet from even Gordon was significant. I guess I had slept for almost thirty minutes when the ward lights were switched on and a lady wearing a white overall stood at the end of my bed and offered me a cup of tea in a jaded plastic blue beaker. I declined with a wave of my hand and a polite 'No Thanks.' I was beginning to feel as though I was being softened up for an interrogation myself.

As I lay dazed by the lights and my own fatigue, my concerns for the woman to my left were interrupted by the noises from the woman to my right. As conscientiously as any proud man after an 8 pint session, she pushed a fart out of her body with the force of a horse. "Oh, that's better" she mumbled. Within a few seconds she coughed which immediately forced another ripping stream of gas in to our atmosphere. She cleared her throat and sniffed. "By dear me," she stated as she responded to the growing sulphurous odour no doubt escaping from her sheets. I wanted to shout 'I'm a celebrity get me out here' as I felt I had subjected myself to sufficient NHS style bush tucker trials to enable me some freedom back to reality. No sooner had she finished her customary morning salutations than she began a diabolical monologue. "Ooh now, what did I say I'd do? Ooh, yes, Donald. No, Mary, maybe, yes." She was clearly rather hard of hearing, as she conducted herself as though she was alone, and at a level where you could have clearly heard her two wards away. And so at the unearthly hour of 6.45 am she began calling various members of her family at the top of her voice. "Hello Love, it's me. I know, it is isn't it. But I'm awake now you see. Yes. Well I'm feeling better. Terrible wind though. I didn't tell you last night but I've got a discharge. No. They said it were alright. How's Timmy? Is he ok? He don't like windows. Best keep curtains drawn. No, I'm on this phone you pay credit on. I watched telly last night. Coronation Street were on. What's her name? You know that one that has funny red hair, she were in it a lot." And so it went on for what seemed like hours. When it wasn't Mary it was Donald and if not him someone else. Eventually a nurse appeared to see her. "Mrs Wilkinson you are a bit loud love" "Hey you what, I'm on the phone you know to Trudy, I've got a discharge, but Malcolm's picking me up you know." "Yes Mrs Wilkinson, but I'm not sure the whole world wants to know." "Hey you what? Hang on Trudy the nurse wants me for sumetts." "Your hearing aid, Mrs Wilkinson, have you turned it on?" Clearly she hadn't. Once she had registered the fact and after a brief pause and a "that's better" she set off talking to Trudy about the important issues of the day. I was sure Trudy was as relieved as I was that it was at a considerably quieter level. It was just like a hospital version of Faulty Towers.

After a while a nurse again attended Mrs Wilkinson. "How's it going love? You home today?" "Yes. Malcolm's picking me up. He's me toy boy you know." "Really?" enquired the nurse. "Yeah, had him for the last 23 year. He's a bit quiet really. He likes to go down pub on his own. It don't bother me like. I don't like pubs anyway. I don't drink. Like to keep fit you know." The nurse politely interrupted Mrs Wilkinson with an occasional "Oh" or a "Really" as she rattled on about Malcolm. "The first time I had him were in 1980. Frank wasn't up to much by then, bless him. Hmm, he died the next year. Malcolm were quite cute then to be fair. Mind you he's gone off a bit recent. He's a fat little bugar really. He were only 45 when I met him you know. Not bad for a 55 year old eh? Mind you the little sod never asked me to marry him. Not sure I'd have said yes anyway. " So it went on and on and on. "I like to watch Coronation Street when he goes to the pub. There's sometimes a toy boy on it an all. What was that girl called? You know! Now who used to be on Coronation Street, you know ran the pub."

What I didn't realise was that at this stage she was opening up the conversation to the entire ward. An elderly man opposite her piped up " What her with the long blonde hair? Judy Goodyears?" "No" said the nurse "you mean Julie Goodyear." "No not her. Before her" "Raquel?" Mrs Wilkinson chipped in. "No" "You mean Vera?" piped up the lady in the far left corner who had only preceded this event by mumbling infrequently about her cat. "No" "Bet Lynch" added the man in the corner. "No, that's same as Julie what's her name." "I know who you mean" said the nurse, "Liz McDonald". "No she weren't a landlady." "I know, "said Mrs Wilkinson, "I've remembered, it was Annie Walker." "Oh, her" everyone exhaled. I closed my eyes, shook my head and wished aliens would abduct me.

Having subjected us all to a SAGA style version of 'Telly Addicts', Mrs Wilkinson elected to break wind again. "Ooh I think I better get off to the loo." As the nurse reversed out of her bay having decided she had spent long enough with Mrs Wilkinson I was amazed to finally get a visual on this incredible woman. She was in her late 70's with enough make up on to hold up the tower of pisa and the brightest bleached blonde hair you have ever seen. As she proceeded along the ward with the nurse in front of her she began rattling on about her toy boy and how he didn't mind her breaking wind as actually he was a lot worse than she was. "Mind you" she said as she reached 'Cat woman's bed' "I've always had an uppity tummy. When we were girls in the war I was always making a noise in the shelter. They didn't know if it were me or the Germans."

There really wasn't much you could say to that.

God.

To be in a position of authority involves a range of important responsibilities not least in the health service. They say a doctor knows everything but does nothing, a consultant knows nothing and does everything, a psychiatrist knows nothing and does nothing and a pathologist knows everything but always a week too late. I had always and somewhat naively assumed that representing the interests of the patient and curing people of their illnesses whilst minimising their discomfort would be the chief priorities of any senior office holder in the NHS. I had no clear understanding of the hierarchical nature between incumbent Consultants in a General Hospital. I was unfortunately unaware of the lack of respect consultants and doctors showed their patients. I was, alas, inexperienced enough to believe that when they came to work, consultants became focused on the people they had been educated and remunerated to serve. My experience was limited and dependent upon a matter of a few minutes of first hand familiarity. Up to the point of Mrs Wilkinson's entertaining rendition, I had encountered just those few moments with Con I back in the isolation room. My mother had in her diligent and adversarial fashion canvassed for me to be seen by a more appropriate consultant and one with a degree of gastroenterological experience. In the interim I had heard nothing from a Doctor, Nurse or Consultant as to whether these heartfelt requests had been addressed. I was no better informed as to whether I was to see a different consultant or be transferred to either a private hospital or be seen under private consultation within this hospital. I was confident therefore that when I recognised Con 1's imposing voice discussing another patient's conditions with a nurse at the door of our ward at breakfast time, I would be receiving some information quite soon.

Con 1 seemed however to have other things on his mind. Despite the considerable evidence of a number of very sick people only a matter of a few yards from his prominent position where he held active debate with the nursing staff, it was clearly not his intention to enter the ward. As he waxed lyrical on his busy schedule another Consultant joined him. Con 2 had a quieter voice and sounded subservient to the apparently superior Con1. "I've had various requests for me to transfer a Charles Davey to you. You heard anything?" asked Con 1 indignantly. My ears pricked up. There was clearly a shrug of the shoulders or some expressive reply as Con 2 didn't comment. Con 1 carried on, "I can't see the point. His parents have become involved and they have tried to get him to be seen privately. I'm not happy with this patient's family trying to push this case through to private. I don't think it's in anyone's interests for that to happen. Agreed?" Con 2 offered a weak, "Mmm, ok." "I'm not transferring him to you either. He's had a bleed and a subsequent transfusion so I shall keep him under me. Blood pressure isn't stable yet and haemoglobins need monitoring. I can't see the point at this stage in him being transferred, can you?" "No" replied Con 2 equally as feebly. "If we moved him to private he wouldn't have the facilities so he can stay here," concluded Con 1 in an authoritative manner. With that my fate was sealed and they drifted into a conversation regarding another matter as they set off up the passage. I was quite amazed that I had been able to over hear their conversation. It seemed highly unprofessional to be discussing my case within earshot of other patients. They clearly had no idea where I was, nor the fact that I could hear their every word. I was frustrated that Con 1 had clearly taken no action towards either enabling me to be seen privately or being transferred to Con 2. I was fascinated to understand what facilities would not be available to me at the private hospital down the road. I was conscious of the 'God' like attitude Con 1 had displayed. I felt that throughout his commanding conversation with Con 2 he had failed to serve my best interests. I wondered what incentives beyond pure medical reasoning directed him towards such a decision. I suspected internal politics and a big chip on his shoulder accounted for a good deal of his audacity. Whether I was under him or Con 2 would have had no influence as to my day to day care or the monitoring of my condition. From the outset I was confident that I was suffering from some internal bowel complaint. My heart was doing a good job and as far as I could establish you didn't need a medical degree to figure out my blood pressure and blood problems were as a result of having lost a lot of blood. I was clear in my own mind as to what course of treatment I needed. The sooner I was under a gastroenterologist who conducted some exploratory examinations of my digestive system the better.

As I lay there my frustration was fuelled by going back over their conversation. The more I thought about it the more annoyed I became. A lovely little story popped into my head and I managed the briefest of smiles;

"Out of my window I saw six men kicking and punching my consultant as he was leaving the hospital. The patient in the next bed said to me are you going to help? No I said, no, six should be enough."

I picked up the phone, checked I had enough phone credit and called home. Mum answered. After various concerns and discussions about my immediate well being, I was able to offload my story about what I had listened to. I spoke very quietly as I was terrified of being overheard. I didn't want to be the one who was always seen as complaining. Mum was equally amazed and a little apprehensive. We were fortunate that within our group of family friends we had a great friend who was an eminent consultant and general surgeon. She had already enquired to him about the various personalities within the hospital whom he knew well. It was his opinion that I should and could be seen by Con 2 if we wanted to be and that there was no reason why I should not be seen privately if I so wished. This very much backed up our gut reactions and re emphasised the strange relationships we had so far encountered with the consultants at the General Hospital. She promised to do some more digging and to call me back later.

I realised that throughout the so far busy morning I had hardly taken account of my surroundings. My curtains were still firmly pulled up each side although the end of the bed was open to the ward. I could barely make out 'Cat woman' in the far corner. I had a full view of Gordon continuing to struggle in his bed. Mrs Wilkinson was behind the curtain to my right and silent for the present. She had decided to switch her television on. A man to Gordon's left remained out of sight and the lady to my left for the moment remained calm. The bustle of a morning in hospital had begun with a new team coming on shift. I hadn't seen my archangel depart. Her absence was significant. It was with considerable trepidation that I pressed my nurse's bell. A smart middle aged sister came to my bed within a few minutes. I obviously looked a state as she immediately set to work straightening me up. "Have you had your blood pressure checked recently?" "Err, no." She set off to find the various instruments. On her return she unhooked my blood transfusion pump and bags and snapped the top of my canula shut. "Would it be possible to use the loo " I asked hopefully. "Sorry no, I shall bring you some more trays, Ok?" I didn't bother answering. Once she had finished checking my observations and before she left I asked her to close my curtain.

As I climbed out of the bed and stood next to my IV stand to relieve myself in to various bits of cardboard, my self-worth crumbled in to dust and rubble. The embarrassment I suffered from these actions in these surroundings seemed wholly inappropriate for a 21st century hospital. I couldn't imagine doing anything more degrading. The noise of fluid hitting hard cardboard and then fluid on fluid was difficult to disguise. Apart from anything else one could see I was standing up from under my curtain. The smell from using my second piece of cardboard was as offensive as if you were in a jail during the middle ages. I rang the bell again as soon as possible to enable a swift removal of everything.

I had been back in bed for a few minutes when I heard the familiar tones of Con 1 approaching. I was not in the mood to see him. I had barely recovered from over hearing his earlier conversation and I was full of trepidation as to how I would react. My brain wasn't working too well and I had barely overcome the indignity of my morning's expulsions. I was without sleep, deeply concerned about my underlying health issues which had now swung away from dysentery to something yet to be explained and as a result of overhearing their conversation somewhat distrustful of the consultants in the hospital.

As a nurse attended to me and removed my unpleasant cardboard offerings Con 1 sailed into view surrounded by a faction of various junior doctors and an odd registrar. They all piled into my limited bay and then pulled the curtain around themselves. I suddenly lay surrounded by several people. I felt as though I was in a freak show. Whereas I had expected a one to one honest and frank discussion at a personal level with a consultant it appeared now I was about to be the centre of some profound demonstration. Con I stood nearby to my right. A registrar stood at the end of my bed with the clip board in his hand and the various minions filled whatever space was left. It was all I could do to keep my head above ground and not pull the covers over my face. "Ok" he started, "This guy has had Melina, been bleeding for about 3 days; Right?" he turned and directed the question to me. "Err, no, no, actually not 3 days," I replied. It was clear that I wasn't going to be a nodding patient. Con I looked at me with an arrogant expression, and then with condescending and superior articulation, said "Sure?" "Oh yes sure." I explained, "I came in through A & E at 1.30 am on Tuesday morning. It's now Wednesday morning. I started bleeding at about 1 pm on the Monday. Not quite two days." "Ok, colour of the Melina?" At this point I had to stop myself from suggesting that if he wanted to look at colours perhaps he could inspect the dozen or so samples I had been forced to produce under somewhat embarrassing circumstances throughout the previous 24 hours. "Blackish", I replied. "Right, let me feel your abdomen. Pull your sheets down, that's it. " His cold hands pressed firmly all over my stomach and abdomen. "Any pain anywhere?" Again I had to resist temptation as in my mind I could hear the words "Yes, you, you bastard!" being formulated but somehow as my mouth opened a straight forward "No" came out. "How many units of blood have you received?" As he asked me he turned to his underlings, "Blood transfusion last night, Haemoglobin low, blood pressure low." "2 units," I answered. "Tell me" he asked, "How much alcohol are you drinking?" I was flabbergasted. "Sorry?" I uttered an almost apologetic question in disbelief. "I want to know your drinking habits." I was appalled. I glanced around at a group of judgemental bastards who were far more interested in determining a simple cause to my predicament rather than trying to find out what may be the medical reason for my complaint. I guessed it would be interesting to know what their drinking habits were too. "Recently as it has been Christmas, lots of parties etc. I guess I've been averaging 20 units per week. But it's hit and miss. Some days nothing and then one night out maybe 8 – 10 units. " I tried my best to morally defend my social activity. It felt like being on trial. "Normally less than that, I guess maybe up to 10 units per week." "Ok" he started, "What we probably have here is a gastric ulcer. Bit of over doing it" He smiled in a supercilious way. I was beginning to think that he made a decision about me which had the tag of 'Time waster, self abuser' written all over it. I was mortified that anyone in his position could be so judgemental without any facts. I couldn't understand how he had shifted from dysentery to stomach ulcer with so little to go on. "We will send you down for an endoscopy later this afternoon. Nil by mouth today. We will go from there." " Would it be possible to see a consultant privately? " I weakly asked. You could cut the atmosphere with a knife. "No point at this stage. You are in the queue. You won't be seen any quicker. Once this test is done we will know more. You will remain under the NHS for now." He looked at me with a confrontational stare. I felt I was on a sticky wicket and I wasn't really feeling like a fight. I shrugged, accepting his opinion. He raised his finger in a departing gesture and the curtain swished round. Con 1 and his team moved on to the next case. I lay there wondering how on earth anyone could take any confidence in their care with a Consultant who had such an appalling bedside manner. I realised that I had, as yet, been unable to find an opportunity to explain a 20 year experience with IBS, a series of tests under a previous consultant 3 years ago investigating potential Crohn's and a GP who if asked would explain regular visits from me over the years complaining about digestive discomfort. How anyone with this person's degree of responsibility in the care of patients could be allowed to operate in this manner was beyond me. Surely asking questions about my medical history, examining the answers to all of the questions I had already been asked by other doctors and understanding the sequence of events that had occurred to me before and after my bleed would be more valuable than stating I was an irresponsible drinker. At that moment I took such a dislike to Con 1 that I became determined to be transferred away from his care at whatever cost. I suddenly felt so sorry for all of the people who found themselves under his control and I wanted to make sure I wasn't one of them.

The team of opinionated social commentators had moved in to the bay next door to interrogate the poor lady who had been promised she may go home. Con 1 was firing similar questions at her as the other doctor's had during the night. She hardly dare speak. She sounded so timid and scared. Her condition remained a mystery despite their badgering and she too was promised tests later in the day. This of course led to her enquiries about going home. She had been promised! There was no way she was going home. As they left her she began to cry again.

Once I was confident that they had departed and were out of ear shot I called home. Mum answered again and after reporting in she promised to find out more as soon as possible to enable me to make a change of consultant if nothing else. She was busy clearing breakfast away. I had not been allowed breakfast and after hearing that she would be in to see me later I lay there thinking about how long it was since I last ate anything and realised it was 48 hours ago. Strangely I didn't feel hungry, just very tired.

Visitors.

By mid morning I was beginning to feel down in the dumps. At 11.15 am I should have been sat in front of an interviewing panel in London chasing a once in a lifetime opportunity. Instead I was trapped in an Institution I had little respect for under the control of a man I held in contempt. I was no nearer finding out what was wrong with me and I felt physically drained. I began questioning the unfairness of life but managed to stop my self-pitying when I noticed Gordon going through a particularly bad episode of struggling in his bed. I wasn't sure what his condition was although I had heard a diabetic coma being mentioned. I felt very bad for being so introverted. I wished Gordon well.

The lady to my left had an impromptu visit from her husband. He sounded like he wanted to be somewhere else. He was condescending and authoritative. No wonder she was so unhappy. All she wanted was some love and support. It sounded to be in short supply and despite her pitiful requests he wasn't interested in taking her home or trying to find out what was the matter with her. He kept telling her that she was in the best place and that the hospital would sort her out. He obviously hadn't met the consultants. He was a complete mood hoover. The last bastion of optimism was sucked out of the room by his presence. He raised his voice to make his points and barely considered the questions she asked in relation to her children back at home. Her tears returned. I looked over at Gordon struggling and my mood deteriorated further. I had never understood until then how depressing Hospitals could be.

The sister who had been to see me earlier in the day drifted down the ward. My IV bag was empty again and she moved towards it. "Hi, how are you doing?" I didn't answer. I heard her, but couldn't summon the energy to explain how I felt. "You seem a bit down." I looked up at her. I had no idea how I looked, but as I was without a shave for three days and without sleep or food for two days and nights I guessed it didn't look good. Gordon moaned opposite and the lady next door sobbed. I looked hard at the sister. Despite being unsure about explaining how I felt, I started, "I'm very frustrated as I seem to be getting nowhere with my requests to be seen either privately or by another consultant." She looked quizzically at me as if to infer that I shouldn't be worrying about such things. I spent a few minutes detailing what had happened and how I wanted to be seen by Con2 as he was the gastroenterologist. Ideally I wanted him to conduct my exploratory procedures in order to see first hand what my condition was like. She listened intently.. "Oh, well I will have a word and see what I can do. I will speak to the consultants when they come round. Don't worry; Chin up." She smiled at me. It was as reassuring as I could hope for and I thanked her. She changed my IV bag and went about her duties.

In truth I didn't hold out much hope. Con I didn't seem to me to be the sort of person who might be persuaded by a ward sister.

Time ticked by. Ladies in blue overalls arrived offering drinks and lunch, neither available to me of course. Mrs Wilkinson's toy boy arrived to collect her. He appeared to be in his 80's despite Mrs Wilkinson's affirmation of him being late 60's. He was the oldest looking toy boy I had ever seen. Malcolm was almost molested by Mrs Wilkinson upon his arrival and he was treated to the various crazy stories she recounted to him about her stay. She of course repeatedly told him about her 'discharge'. I couldn't help but smile and she did more to lighten the mood in the ward than anyone. Once they departed the place became quiet and sombre.

I was delighted to see Mum arrive at about 2.30pm. She was breezy and upbeat. She had managed to talk to our family friend who had once again encouraged me to advance my requests to be seen by Con 2 if I wasn't happy to be seen by Con 1. In his opinion there was absolutely no reason why I shouldn't make such a request and it be met. My GP had also enquired about me and was dutifully concerned. He was available to talk to and had promised to do whatever he could to help. She brought many well wishes from various people. I was staggered as to how many people had contacted her to enquire about my well being. Martin had called her to explain the position that the Nuffield scholarship trust had reached. It appeared they were fully behind me. They recognised a credible scholar and they wanted me on board if at all possible. Dependent upon my recovery and subsequent health they were, under the circumstances, prepared to set up an individual interview so that I could still make Calgary in February. As she talked about how much they wanted me, I felt a lump develop in my throat. Emotional and tired, I felt tears fill my eyes. Somehow I stopped them from running down my face. It was the singularly most uplifting and encouraging moment in the last three days and as Mum left, promising to return later in the day, I felt as though there was a glimmer of hope and that my trip of a life time might still be on.

Not long after she had gone the sister came back to check my blood pressure and other vital signs. "I think you will be moved to another ward this afternoon. I'm not sure about your endoscopy though. I think it might be delayed.

I have tried to get you moved to another consultant's list. No joy yet though." She checked my IV made sure I had everything I needed to hand and set off back to her station.

Within a few minutes a new Doctor, Doc 6, arrived at my bedside. He asked the obligatory 20 questions. I was confused as to what his role was and how he fitted in to the day to day care. He asked me how I felt and asked for some more blood tests to be taken. The sister duly arrived and took several more blood samples away. Hancock had nothing on me.

At about 4pm Sister returned to inform me that she had managed to arrange my movement to Con 2's ward. This didn't necessarily mean I would be seen by him but at least I was on the ward with the rest of his designated patients. It felt like a minor victory and I was surprised that the sister had managed where everyone else seemed to have failed. Sure enough within a few minutes a porter arrived to move me. He pushed a wheel chair to the edge of my bed. The sister disconnected my drip. All of my belongings were bagged up which the sister carried for me. The porter wheeled me out of the admissions ward and turned left. There was increased corridor noise as I experienced the phones, chatter and hustle and bustle of people moving about. Within 20 yards we turned left in to another ward. To my immediate left as we came through the door there was a freshly made bed. The porter parked me up and the sister dropped off my bag of belongings. As she did so a happy voice acknowledged my arrival," Hello love, how are you doing? I'm Rosie." The new Sister was engaging and fun from the outset. She interacted with all of her patients. Within 5 minutes of my arrival she had introduced me to everyone on the ward. Barry, David, Colin and Arthur all said "Hello" and waved to me from their beds. Harold to my immediate left didn't move. He was asleep. His white hair and pale face combined with his rasping breathing indicated that saying 'Hello' was a bit beyond him at present. His 70 + years were not out of place however. I was the youngest on the ward by some considerable distance. The average age of the remainder of the ward was about 65. As I made myself comfortable in my 4th bed within 36 hours Rosie fussed around me. It felt great to be the centre of attention. "Would you like something to eat or drink?" she asked. I explained that I was hoping to still go down for an endoscopy. "When did you last have something to eat?" I explained it was Monday morning at breakfast some two and a half days ago. "Right, well I better go and find out what's happening. Don't want you wasting away whilst they decide what they are doing." With that and a big smile she paced out of the ward and left me to my own devices. I set up my TV with my credit card and took in my surroundings. It was a replica ward to the last except that it was all male. Most of the inmates seemed to have been here a while as they had far more paraphernalia surrounding their beds. There were 'Get well' cards, newspapers, magazines, bowls of fruit and assorted drinks next to their bedsides. My own contribution seemed meagre rations in comparison. One copy of Lincolnshire Life, an out of date 'Evening Telegraph' and a book I had no great intention to read. I knew however that Mother was on her way back in at some point with various other books and some personal effects which would get me on par. By about 5.30 pm I was beginning to wonder what was going to happen to me and I was delighted when Rosie returned. "They've still got a few to do so you won't be going down today." She could see I was a bit disappointed. "Don't worry, I think you can have a drink; I shall bring you some water and maybe a bit of food. Do you think you could eat?" I thought about it. "Maybe although I'm not sure what I can eat. What I would really like is a bath or a shower. Would that be ok?" "Of course love, when did you last have one?" "Three days ago." "Ooh, poor thing. You get ready and I will show you where to go." I didn't have much to get ready; a toothbrush, a razor and a few toiletries was all I could muster. Rosie brought a towel and some soap. I climbed out of bed and started to follow her. I was amazed at how slow I was across the floor under my own mobilisation. I felt very weak. "You ok love?" "Fine." There was no way I was going to be prevented from cleaning myself up. As I entered the bathroom and before I closed the door I asked about using the loo. "Of course you can love." As I slid the lock across I realised that this was the first time in three days that I was on my own and under my own management. Being allowed to sit on a loo seemed a luxury. It was an incredibly empowering moment. It felt like you were establishing control back in to your life. At the same time I realised how more dependent people than me must feel about losing their independence forever. As inspiring a moment as it was, my feet were kept firmly on the ground with this sobering thought. I looked in the mirror. I barely recognised the pale and gaunt face staring back at me. Dark rings surrounded my listless eyes. Three days of stubble set off my down turned expression. The white gown covered in hospital crosses institutionalised the complete effect. I looked awful. I rubbed my face, sighed and set about trying to re-establish the old me. Half an hour later I felt a lot better. Shaved and clean I put the gown back on. I still looked ill but at least I was presentable.

I had been back in my bed about 10 minutes when a familiar face appeared at the door. My best mate Ian looked at me, trying to establish whether I might live or die. He smiled, "You're still here then?" He cracked a smile a mile wide which was infectious. He had arrived bearing gifts which included a very funny card involving nurses and breasts which had been very carefully signed by his three year old daughter, who conveyed many kisses and loves for

Uncle Ed. It was a great feeling to see him. He was full of stories about various people sending their best wishes and concerns. We talked about rugby, work and women as well as hospitals. I explained some of what had happened and he listened intently. He was desperate to find out whether I had spotted any decent nurses. I told him about Angels and Archangels. We decided there probably was a God as a result. Laughter filled our bay. On top of my recent move to the new ward, my recent ablutions and my visit had improved the way I felt enormously. Rosie turned up with some fresh water. It tasted like champagne. I thanked her. Within a few minutes Mother and Father turned up and suddenly I had more company than I had seen for days. They told me that my sister would come and see me tomorrow morning and that she would bring me some new pyjamas and slippers. The value of all of the visits was measured by the company and conversation and having the people who you cared about most spending their time with you. It was as important a tonic as anything the hospital or medical staff could do. Over the next few days I learnt more about the other patients on the ward. I grew to understand how fortunate I was in comparison to some of them. Barry, along the ward, only received one visit a fortnight from his brother. He was divorced and his remaining family either lived too far away or had passed on. His closest relatives were either dead or unable to be with him. I often thought of Barry every time someone sat next to my bed. It must be an even greater challenge to live through hospitalisation without the support of your closest friends and family. I was in admiration of the way he managed his illness and the challenges he had to face alone. Over the forthcoming days I was to receive visits from my girlfriend, aunties, friends as well as my close family including nephews and nieces. It was without doubt the most comforting and enjoyable period whilst in hospital. For any patient knowing you are not alone means the most.

A new nurse arrived at my bedside once they had all departed and informed me that I was to have my endoscopy at 11 am tomorrow and so I would remain without food. I asked who would conduct it and she said that it would be under Con 2. I assumed he would agree to see me privately once I had the chance of meeting him. I was delighted. Somehow in the back room of the hospital I had been transferred away from Con 1. Under the circumstances not having anything to eat seemed a small price to pay as in my head I celebrated my minor victory. As evening descended I felt exhaustion tugging at me. For the first time in three days I fell in to an untroubled sleep which lasted for hours.

Gastroscopy.

I was woken up at 6 am with a start. The lights were switched on in a 'National Service' type reveille. I expected to have to jump out and stand by my bed in early morning military formation. A lady in blue overalls pushed a tea trolley (circa 1960's) along the ward. "Tea love?" For the first time in a while I accepted. "Milk love? Sugar love?" "Please, " I chirped. The chipped blue plastic mug contained the first warm drink I had consumed in days and was very welcome. As I looked around the ward it was clear that everyone else was struggling with the wakeup call too. A round of "Morning" was passed along the ward as each of us recognised the other. One felt a sort of relief that we'd made it through the night. A band of brothers!

By the time Rosie and crew started their shift and arrived on the ward with their accustomed gusto and smiles it had transpired that there was some doubt about when I might be taken for my endoscopy. Since my sister was planning on coming in to see me from a fair distance away I thought I better keep her informed. I relayed the problem to her by phone explaining that I wasn't sure when I was going down to receive the procedure. I had hoped to be back on the ward by the time visiting hours started at 2 pm but now there was a degree of uncertainty. As a result my cup of tea proved to be the last bit of joy for some time as I was to be nil by mouth from then on regardless of when the endoscopy might take place. I kept my fingers crossed that it would be 11 am and that Con 2 was a reliable timekeeper.

As 11 am crept up it seemed ever less likely that I was going to be called. I had watched Arthur receive various preps for his procedure. It was something to do with an exploratory investigation on his heart. His wife had sat by his bedside throughout the pre –op. I wondered what was going through her mind. As I waited, I learnt more about the other patients on the ward. Crohn's, diabetes, digestive disorders, pneumonia and other cardiopulmonary issues covered most of our conditions. It seemed that whatever I was suffering from it was on one of the more serious lists.

11 am came and went and so I asked for more news. There was none. I had my blood pressure taken and I was asked to make sure that I continued using bits of cardboard even in the loo. I had another set of blood tests taken. Time drifted on. Lunchtime came and went and I still hadn't been called. Arthur was wheeled back in still under his anaesthesia.

At 2pm Sarah turned up with the promised various bedclothes. It was lovely to see her. As a practising pharmacist she was intrigued as to how my treatment was progressing. She was somewhat surprised to hear my tale to date and that I was so far no further on to finding out what was wrong with me. She was extremely concerned about me, however she was starting, as had my mother when she visited, to follow Con1's line of thinking that it was likely to be a stomach ulcer. In her opinion I had maybe been out too much, drunk too much and had been under a great deal of stress. I was beginning to tire of the judgemental approach people were taking towards my health. Admittedly it had all started with Con 1's opinion in the isolation room. People, particularly visiting relatives and dependents want to know as soon as possible what might be wrong with you.

When someone of alleged credibility indicates a diagnosis people are keen to follow their opinion. I was, however not so keen. I didn't want to accept Con I's or my sister's view and receive this diagnosis lying down. I explained that I wasn't that stressed by all of the episodes and challenges I had faced and I believed I had handled the situations, some of which had been extreme, particularly well under the circumstances. My drinking was no more or less than anyone else I had spent any time with recently and I took exception to being told that I had been effectively over doing it. I had been to some good parties but I had also been going to the gym and eating sensibly. There had been far more days without a drink or a big meal than there ever was with. I hardly represented a bad role model. I had recently noticed a general degree of judgemental behaviour from my immediate family. It appeared they wanted to box up the reason for me being here and that the best line to follow was that of the consultants. I was in no mood to accept either the consultants or my family's opinion of how I ran my life. I remained calm but conscious that some people were too willing to make judgements about me, when we knew absolutely nothing about why I had fallen ill. I knew i was treading on dangerous ground but I was convinced that what had happened to me was not a stomach ulcer or a social illness. Despite our slight difference of opinion I still really enjoyed her visit and the ward was a far more boring place when she left an hour later.

As my thirst and hunger grew so did my frustration. The hours ticked by. Sue occasionally checked the running schedule for me but always came back with the answer, "Not sure." Out of the blue and without announcement a porter arrived at about 4.30pm to take me down for my procedure. He arrived in a flurry of radio commentary back to his manager about arriving at his destination and expected ETA back to base. It all seemed rather dramatic.

I put my dressing gown on over my hospital gown and after he had collected my files from the nurse's station we set off down the corridor.

As I was wheeled along the corridor I wondered what the procedure I was about to undergo would be like. Having an endoscope down your throat didn't sound particularly pleasant. I thought that at least now that I was under Con 2 there was a chance that he would get to the root of the problem. I was looking forward to meeting him and having the chance to discuss my condition. So far no clear diagnosis had been made and although Con 1 had indicated various theories I remained unconvinced about anything he had come up with. The sooner they could find out the cause and the solution, the sooner I could get out of the hospital. That had to be good for both me and the NHS.

I entered a new part of the hospital which had clearly only been built in the very recent past. In comparison to the rest of the building it was clean and bright. The infrastructure and equipment looked in good condition and thoroughly professional. I was dropped off by the porter with his radio squawking about being back in ten. I was met by a nurse who went through a series of admission type questions and then I was left in a waiting room. Time ticked by. By 5.30 pm and as I was beginning to think they had forgotten me, the nurse returned. "Ok, Mr Davey, this way please." She led me along a corridor and through some swing doors into an operating theatre. A Doctor sat at a desk working on a pc. I put out my hand "Hello Doctor, it's good to finally meet you." He looked at me quizzically. "I'm the registrar." He introduced himself. I began to feel a growing sense of unease. I had anticipated meeting Con 2 , talking through my case, listening to what he was going to do during the procedure and then learning about what he had found at the end of it all before I returned to the ward. I also hoped he may be able to give me some idea as to whether I was going to need additional procedural investigations. Instead I was looking at someone I had never heard of. "Right Mr Davey, this is what we are going to do. We will lay you on the bed, give you a mild sedative and then slide the endoscope down your oesophagus. Once we have the endoscope down there we will examine the stomach and then the top of the duodenum. If I see anything down there I will deal with it whilst I'm in there. This may involve pegging, sealing or pinching, Ok?" I was shocked. I was in the company of a man I knew nothing about whom I suddenly had to put my trust in. Up to this point I had assumed that Con 2 would be seeing me, and I understood he was to have conducted the endoscopy. I had never been led to understand that the procedure was anything more than exploratory and I was certainly not expecting to be treated by this procedure and under this registrar. I had wrongly assumed I was going to be given the option of being treated privately. All of these thoughts were going through my mind. I could feel a disturbing frustration and anger stirring in my body and I knew I was about to say something which wouldn't go down very well. My silence filled the room as I thought through all of these issues. It started to concern the medical staff. "Is there a problem?" the registrar asked. "Yes there bloody well is" I exclaimed. The registrar and the two nurses suddenly resembled rabbits in headlights. "I was under the misconception that I was to be treated by a consultant!" I explained my concerns regarding the procedure, the lack of Con2 and my lack of choice about my appropriate care. The nurse's eyes widened. I was given the impression that it wasn't the done thing. The Registrar seemed rather put out. "Mr Davey, I always do these procedures. Your consultant will not be conducting this procedure and you are unable to be seen privately in this hospital. Would you like me to continue?" "No," I remained indignant, "How can you expect me to be prepared to accept that you may well do something to me surgically whilst you are in there with the endoscope when I was never informed that this might be the case? I have been asking to be seen privately for three days, ever since I came in. I believed I was about to meet my consultant and that I would have the opportunity of discussing things with him. I thought this was an investigation to find out what had caused my bleed." It all sort of blurted out. I knew I was close to becoming very angry. "Look Mr Davey, there is a risk to this procedure. If I go in now I want to be able to do the necessary work. Going in a second time is too risky. The only way you could be seen by your consultant is to delay the procedure. There is a risk again to that. You could bleed again at any time. If you delay you might be risking your health." I was staggered. "I've been waiting for 24 hours anyway. I was meant to be seen yesterday. There must have been a risk delaying my procedure as well!" He looked at me with disdain. I was simply not complying. "Look, if your ulcer bursts again you could have another gastric bleed, but it might be worse this time, it might take longer to stop." "I'm sorry" I replied, "But we don't even know whether I have an ulcer." "According to the consultant who has seen you on the ward he believes that it is the most likely cause and this investigation will verify it." By now I was getting really steamed, which wasn't the best thing for a man with a potential ulcer. "He's a cardio consultant. The gastro consultant hasn't even seen me yet, despite repeated requests. How can I make a decision on any of this, with such appalling advice?" "Mr Davey, I can see you are getting upset. Would you like to have a few minutes to think it through? I really do believe it's in your best interests to have it done now by me. I am very good at this procedure. I have years of experience conducting it. You must trust me." I shook my head. "This hospital is on the list of my private medical insurance. I should be able to receive private treatment with a chosen consultant referred by my GP. Why can't this happen?" "Sorry Mr Davey, no private treatment will, has or can be done in this hospital." My chin dropped onto my chest and I sighed. "Mr Davey," one of the nurses piped up, "Come and have a sit down in the waiting room with me and we can talk things through. Let's have a 5 minute think eh?" I looked at her and at the registrar. I shook my head and climbed off the bed and shoved the swing doors open. She led me to an arm chair and indicated that I should sit down. I was shaking. "Let me get you a blanket". She returned momentarily and put the blanket around me. "You need to make a decision as to what you want us to do, ok?" I looked at her. I had dozens of ideas rushing around my head. Most of them were beyond my experience and I needed to be led. The trouble was I wasn't sure I trusted the advice I was receiving. "I want to know whether the consultant will do the procedure please. I assume I'm right in understanding he is the best person in this hospital to do it.?" They concurred and agreed to call him. Within 5 minutes they were back. "He can do it, but it will be either late tomorrow or after the weekend. If you leave it even 24 hours you are taking quite a risk!" I shook my head in disbelief. "It will still be through the NHS though." I sat and racked my mind in an attempt to make the right decision.

The registrar came in to the waiting room. "What do you think? " I looked at him trying to analyse the degree of trust I held him in. I wasn't sure if I trusted him at all. I only met him about half an hour ago, but unless I was prepared to take an unnecessary risk with my health maybe I needed to. But then again, that in itself was maybe a risk. How could I know one way or the other? I considered all of the worst case scenarios and decided that going ahead was more important than anything else. The sooner I got to the bottom of this the better. I plumped up the courage, "Ok,

I'll go ahead." "You've made the right decision," he replied. He disappeared off back to the operating theatre. After about 5 minutes one of the nurses turned up. "Edward, I'm really sorry but we have a problem." I looked up. "Because you have had a blood transfusion we have no cross matches with your blood." I was dismayed, "You're kidding. They've taken loads of blood tests already. Actually my veins are quite bruised, look!" I showed her the grey bruising on both of the insides of my elbows. "Maybe so, but not for cross matching. We need to send some more off to haematology. It will take about an hour before they come back with the result. If we do the procedure without it and you have a bleed we won't have any blood of your type on standby. Sorry." She fetched needles, syringes and blood sample vials and proceeded to extract more blood into 4 different coloured vials. It took an age to find a vein and the eventual flow was very slow. Once she had obtained the samples it occurred to them that it was now 6 pm and they would have to take the samples round to the department personally. A volunteer was needed as the shift end was near and people were thinking about going home. I just sat there in disbelief.

I began to imagine what would have happened if I hadn't kicked up a stink. What if they had done the procedure, then had a problem and then found they were without a blood match. It didn't bear thinking about. My confidence dipped a bit more. As the various staff on the department that were now held up by the wait for the cross checks used the phone I found myself sat through their calls. "Hello Love. Going to be late home, sorry. Yeah, got a patient still to do. Hopefully won't be too long. No, just a difficult end to the day." As I listened to each of them cast their opinion of my impact upon their day to their loved ones I felt evermore guilt ridden. After about half an hour a phone rang at the reception desk. One of the nurses answered it.

"You are kidding!" she exclaimed down the phone, "That's ridiculous. You sure?" It appeared they were. Once the nurse had put the phone down she walked over to me. "Bit of bad news. We need to retake the blood samples. Unfortunately the samples that went up to haematology were in the wrong coloured vials. They need to be in pink topped ones." I looked at her, closed my eyes and shook my head. As I continued to shake I started pulling up my sleeves. She headed off for her equipment. The registrar came back with the strap, needles and vials. He began looking for a vein. I explained that my arm hurt and that the vein he was prodding had been used about a dozen times in the last couple of days. "Sorry, it's the best one you've got!" Eventually, through gritted teeth, a very slow trickle started to run into the vials. I was told I would need to wait for about an hour. I wasn't the only one in ear shot who sighed deeply.

By about 7.45 pm I was getting tired. I had tried to lighten the mood with a few gags and good stories but even the nurses were flagging and laughter was a rare commodity. I began telling various doctor jokes which for a while kept everyone sufficiently amused. Even so everyone was delighted when the news came through that we were ready to go.

I had grown cold and a bit bored through the wait despite my one man show. I had almost forgotten the reason for my visit to the department. As I stood up and walked back into the operating theatre my mind began to race with the various outcomes of the next thirty minutes. As soon as I walked through the door the Registrar proffered a pen towards me. He sat at the same desk from earlier and by his side on the desk was a consent form. "Please read and sign this Mr Davey." I picked it up and started reading it. I particularly liked the bit where it said, "I understand that you cannot give me a guarantee that a particular person will perform the procedure. The person will, however, have appropriate experience." I wondered what was 'appropriate' about this situation. I gave up reading the remainder of the form. It was clear that regardless of what was in it, I had made a decision to go ahead. Everyone was now waiting for me. It occurred to me that it would have been nice to have had the chance to read it during the previous two hours whilst we waited for the cross checks. I didn't bother commenting as such however. I was becoming conscious of the fact that I was about to let this bloke put a long pipe down in to my stomach and duodenum. On the form it stated 'danger of perforation, haemorrhage, reaction, dental damage and aspiration issues' so I elected not to upset him at this stage, as I preferred a steady hand. I scribbled a signature which was considerably more legible than his.

They moved me over to the table and asked me to climb on. The nurses busily prepared various drugs off to one side of the room. The registrar stood before me. "Lay down. Ok we are going to give you a mild sedative. Once that's done we are going to put a clamp between your teeth. I want you to bite firmly on it. The sedative will help reduce your gag reflex whilst I slide the tube in. " My eyes widened with concern, "I've received Rihipnol for a procedure before and it had no effect upon me." I was conscious of them administering sufficient sedative to make a difference. "We'll give you a good shot, don't worry." It hardly sounded scientific but as I was already feeling guilty of delaying things so I resisted commenting further. One of the nurses moved towards me with a syringe. She plugged it in to my canula and dispensed 'the good shot' in to my arm. It felt very cold as it mingled with my blood, little of it though there was. I figured I must now have about a 50/50 mix of sedative and blood pumping around the system. "Ok bite down on this." They pushed a block in to my mouth and I duly applied the required pressure. "Ok we are going to put you on Oxygen." They slid a tube up my nose and I felt a supply of oxygen make itself available. Within seconds the Registrar appeared at my side with the endoscope. Before I could comment on whether I thought the sedative might take a while to take effect I felt the tube irritate the back of my throat and I gagged. Now this wasn't your little sore throat cough, or even your totally pissed up chunder or even your violently ill vomiting type of gag. This was a head jerking, convulsing, 'John Hurt out of alien' type of reaction. I immediately felt like I'd been sectioned as I found two nurses restraining me, one fore and one aft. They held my head tightly. "Try to remain still; it will be all over shortly" they piped up. The tube continued its journey and I continued to violently gag despite my best efforts not to. "Stay calm, think of something nice, it will be over shortly." I somehow didn't believe that thinking of Kylie undressed was going to make much difference as the endoscope carried on its journey. I gagged time and time again. Despite their best efforts the nurses were struggling to keep me still and the registrar was having a battle getting the scope to its destination. After a few minutes he stopped feeding it in. My gag reflex was regular and continually violent. "Ok, a bit longer please." I could feel fluid running down my cheeks as my eyes watered from the discomfort. I couldn't stop my body reacting despite my best attempts. As the nurses continued to hold me, the Registrar tried his best to view the scope's pictures on his screen. After a few more seconds, which felt like hours, he pushed the endoscope a little further. "Ok, just need to have a look in to the duodenum." My gag reflex took on an all new 'Escaping Alien' type convulsion and it was clear that I was in danger of helping the registrar poke a hole through my insides. "Right that's enough, I'm coming out." The relief was intense. The endoscope virtually flew out of my body and I sucked in an enormous amount of air. As I coughed and spluttered I felt rather pathetic and not very brave.

"There's nothing there." As the nurse took the block, through which the endoscope had been fed, out of my mouth I began regaining my composure. "Sorry?" I spluttered. "There's nothing there. Everything is normal. No ulceration. Top of your duodenum is clear as well. It must be lower down. It's good news. Sorry I can't tell you what it is that's causing you your problem, but I can tell you what it isn't. It isn't an ulcer." "So much for Con I" I reflected. I wanted to ask what else it might be. "If it's not a stomach ulcer might it be something more serious?" I posed the question in the hope that I might learn something. "If I was you I would look at this as good news, don't be imagining things you haven't got, ok?" I looked at this man of medicine and thought what a useless jumped up arsehole he really was. It wouldn't have hurt him to have spent a few minutes talking intelligently to me about my condition and what might happen to me now as a result of the outcome of the procedure. I withdrew any further ideas of talking to him and lay back down on to my trolley.

Within minutes I was being wheeled back towards my ward on a trolley by the nurses. I realised that I had just started to become light headed as the sedative kicked in. I considered that now would be a good time to put an endoscope down my throat. As I considered my recent experiences I reviewed what he had done and how I would have done it differently in his place. If I had been conducting the same procedure as the Registrar I would have arranged a preliminary session with my patient probably through the ward sister to explain who would have been conducting the procedure, how long it would take and what would be involved. I would have ironed out any issues relating to the consultant and the private/NHS debate well before I was going to stick a tube down my patient's throat. I would have administered sedatives earlier and checked my patient's progress before conducting the procedure. I would have made sure cross checks had been done on my blood. For someone who reckoned he was experienced he seemed a bit of a prat. I wouldn't have wanted to have met a first timer.

I reached the ward and noticed a clock on the wall reading 8.40 pm. A lot seemed to have happened since I had left at 4 O'clock. Mother and Father were waiting by my bed. It was great to see some friendly faces. Unfortunately I was in no fit state to talk to them. Despite the fact that they had waited a long time for my arrival back on to the ward, within a short time and after some much appreciated concern they left me to rest. I wondered whether everyone had my sort experience in this hospital but I couldn't find the energy to ask Arthur how he had got on. He was asleep anyway. As I lay back on my pillow, I quickly joined him despite the rasping and rattling breathing of Harold only a few feet to my left.

Barry and Friends.

Morning reveille at 6.30 am was almost a lie in. Blue chipped plastic beakers and warm soapy tea accompanied the fully lit ward and rounds of 'Morning Love'. I had slept fitfully as a result of the sedative. My newly acquired sore throat as a result of the endoscope was eased by the warm sugary drink. It occurred to me as I lay there that I had stopped using the bathroom as regularly, but since I had barely consumed anything for 4 days, it was really no surprise. Nonetheless it was clear that my bleed had healed, my impending death was now back on the long term register and I was on the mend. I looked around the ward at my fellow in mates. They were all coping with the regime as best they could. Harold however wasn't yet awake and he still made the irrevocable chesty noise as he breathed in and out. There was a distinct smell of incontinence drifting from his general area and I hoped someone would soon deal with whatever issues lurked behind his curtain. Dave sat up in his bed opposite me. "You ok? Everyone was worried about you last night. You were a long time!" I hadn't realised that I would be missed by my compatriots, particularly as I was the new boy on the block, but it appeared that nonetheless there had been some genuine concern for my absence. As I briefly explained what had happened Dave shook his head and muttered various exclamations of disbelief. By the time I had finished my tea and talked to Dave, I felt fit enough to take the short walk to the shower room.

By the time I returned, breakfast was being pushed around the wards on a trolley with various blue uniformed ladies administering the meal. My weetabix and bread roll with accompanied small portion of spread and marmalade sat on a basic catering tray placed on my bedside table. It resembled a meal from the gods as a result of not eating for the last 104 hours. One of the ladies walking around the ward offered milk and sugar to each and every person to accompany their breakfast cereal. A nurse joined in to help. I watched them take almost fifteen minutes to achieve the task, partly as a result of their intermittent conversation with each other regarding various non work issues. It seemed ludicrous to be employing staff to spend so much of their time shaking a teaspoon of sugar over someone's weetabix or porridge or applying individual portions of milk to each breakfast from a large jug. As I watched them at work a scene out of school from my childhood came to mind when we would be treated in a similar fashion. It seemed an archaic process as well as a waste of expensive resources in an age when catering for institutions had become so sophisticated. Even a small individual jug of milk and a sachet of sugar on each tray made more sense than someone walking around with a communal jug and a bowl of sugar to every bed in the hospital as a separate operation. Before I could begin my time and motion study, Rosie breezed in to the ward. Her enthusiasm for her job and life generally, swept all and sundry before her. Within a few short minutes she transformed a reasonably gloomy atmosphere in to a chatty, happy and bright place to be. It made me realise that nursing wasn't all about direct care. Even so she was competent enough to recognise that poor Harold needed more than a bowl of special K. With a whisk of the curtain and a call to arms from Rosie, a number of nursing staff disappeared into Harold's bay to clean him up. I was very pleased that I'd finished my breakfast.

Once breakfast and whatever Harold had done had been cleared away, I began reading the newspapers that my various visitors had kindly brought along for me. It felt good to begin reconnecting with the outside world. Rosie wandered past, "You ok this morning Edward?" I nodded and smiled. "Not too bad thanks," I replied. She then said something to me which seemed so out of context that I still think about it today, "What do you think to the NHS now? Not so bad is it?" I really couldn't understand why I had been picked out and asked for such an affirmation. Apart from my run in with Con I and the problem I had experienced with the Registrar I had not actually made any reference to being seen privately and I certainly hadn't made any bold statement about the deficiencies of the NHS to anyone. I had discussed things with the other ward sister before I was moved and I guessed that this was where the comments had come from. By the very nature of her question it appeared that I had been talked about at some level as being a malcontent in regard to NHS care. It was either that or they were just good at reading people. I was rather disappointed that they felt a need to pass judgement on me. No sooner had I engrossed myself in considering this issue and whilst I trawled through an article about the financial ineptitude of the NHS, of all things, I was interrupted by a new blue overall clad lady with a different trolley. "Can I take your old newspapers love?" "What old newspapers?" I enquired. "You don't want all of them, you'll never read 'em," she declared. Without hesitation she moved towards my bedside table to begin sorting through my pile of assorted daily rags. "Excuse me," I blurted out, "What are you doing exactly?" She looked at me and smiled, "Which ones do you think you want to keep then?" "Well, all of them, thanks," I answered. "Well you'll not have room soon," she observed mockingly as she continued to finger the pile of papers and magazines my friends and family had so far dropped off. "Ooh, I reckon I might get through all of these today. Look, come back another time when I've read them please, ok!" "Can't I have some love?", she clearly wasn't going to drop it. "Er, No!" I restated. "Why don't you read a nice book instead?" I was probably rude and abrupt but I was aghast at her audacity. "Just leave my papers where they are thanks. I'll read them in my own time, not yours!" She had decided that I was clearly incapable of reading news print and should spend more time watching daytime TV or reading Jilly Cooper. I stared hard at her as she continued to finger the top copies. Eventually she took the sensible option and decided from my continuing challenging stare that I was not backing down. She smiled awkwardly, backed away from my bedside table and moved along to pester another inmate with a "You'll not want all of those will you love?" I began to wonder who set the work schedules for these people. It was like being in an institution where all of your freedoms of choice were taken away and 'Big Brother' made all of your decisions for you. How much sugar, how much milk, how many news papers! It was absurd.

After no more than a few minutes of undisturbed reading I was distracted by some activity just outside the ward. "Rosie, are you about?" A nurse from another ward had come down to the nurse's station just outside our door. "We've got to move some patients. There aren't enough on his ward next door. He wants three from yours." 'Him' turned out to be my old mate, Con 1. "What do you mean he wants three?" enquired Rosie. "He says he needs three, any three, moving back to his ward ASAP." I felt a moment of dread as I realised one of them could be me. My ears pricked up. Sal, another nurse, joined the discussion. As the situation was re explained a lot of exasperated comments flowed from the assembled audience. "God, sometimes I get really fed up with this," one of them exclaimed, "Why doesn't anyone coordinate what they are doing. It's crap. He shouldn't suddenly request patients just like that. We've got enough to do." Another voice joined in, "They were probably only moved yesterday some of them, now moved again, it's ridiculous. Why should we be wasting our time moving patients about just cos he wants it?" Rosie's voice rose above the others again, "Ok, usual thing too many blinking targets; let's get on with it." Silence descended and the bustle of moving bodies broke up the meeting. Within a few minutes I heard reorganisation in the ward one up from ours. Two were being selected from there. Rosie and Sal came in to our ward and patrolled the aisle clearly considering who was for the chop. None of the other in mates seemed to have a clue as to what was going on. After a quick mid ward chat they headed over to Colin to tell him the good news. Within the space of twenty minutes he had been packed up and shipped out. Little wonder visitors never found the patients they came to visit. They were never in the same place long enough for anyone visiting to get their bearings.

By mid morning I was beginning to produce a large pile of read news papers which I knew would make someone happy. I couldn't help but notice two attractive young women who walked into the ward and headed down to the far end where Barry lay. It became clear that they were the Hospital dieticians. They asked him various questions about his recent eating habits and discussed a few results with him. I could hear Barry complaining about his diet and about the discrepancy which lay between what he should consume and what the hospital catering facility actually delivered for him to eat. My opinion of them dipped somewhat as I observed their approach to dealing with Barry. The more he asked the less he seemed to get. They clearly intended to impose their ideas rather than discuss any of his concerns with him. As their conversation developed it became clear that his opinion was disapproved of as their condescension increased. After they had finished talking to him and as they left the ward they had to walk past my bed. They were completely unaware that I was watching them. One of them rolled her eyes, slightly shaking her head, "It's a good job we don't have too many of those!" she whispered. "Isn't he awful" said the other. I was appalled.

It took a while for it to sink in. Here were girls of about 25 years of age employed on a salary of maybe £20,000 a year doing a job actually partly funded by the very patient they were treating. There appeared to be no understanding of this relationship, no compassion, no care and certainly no respect. They had put themselves up the pecking order. They only cared about their wellbeing rather than what should have been the very focus of their role within the hospital, the patient's wellbeing. I would until that point have welcomed a dietician's input. I was suffering from a complaint which one would consider to be typical of the type of condition which would benefit from dietary advice. I had not and in fact never did throughout my entire experience benefit from any such advice from any of the medical team handling my case. Having seen the type of person who would have delivered this advice had it been offered I was pleased I sought my own advice elsewhere eventually. I was appalled at the lack of interest in Barry's case from these dieticians. In his particular circumstances the advice and input from someone with their training could make an enormous difference to his health and recovery. It made me wonder what these girls held in their heads as far as ideas about job satisfaction. I suspected drinking vodka shots, dancing around their hand bags and who was on their 'shag' list filled their cotton wool heads most of the time.

After I while I calmed down and just as I was about to tackle a broadsheet I was surprised by the arrival of the registrar who had conducted my endoscopy along with

Con2. They immediately pulled the curtain around my bed and as I had never yet met him, Con 2 moved across and introduced himself. My first impression was of a reserved, thoughtful character with a considerably better bed side manner than Con1. I was duly impressed.

Once the formalities had been dealt with Con 2 asked the registrar to describe the observations he had made during the endoscopy. As there was little to report it didn't take long. Con 2 shifted his attention back to me. After asking after my general health which seemed to be slowly improving he asked more specific questions about my recent illness. Not once did he refer to my social life, drinking habits or marital status. He questioned me about my recent symptoms and a brief history with IBS. He was interested to hear about a previous investigation with another consultant in the past. He asked the most exact information about my recent symptoms from my overall well being through to how long the bleed episode lasted and the exact colour of the Melina. I felt as though there was a genuine interest in my condition for the first time since I had arrived in the hospital nearly five days earlier. He spent nearly 10 minutes examining me, pressing on various parts of my stomach and abdomen. Once he had finished his examination he looked me in the eye, "We need you to remain in for observation. On Monday I want to do a colonoscopy, right?" "Ok" I replied. "Depending on what we find I shall then send you for a camera capsule, probably down to Harley Street, ok?" I nodded as this all sounded too good to be true. "I want this sorting out as fast as possible; we need to be cautious about which investigatory procedures we follow but we need some answers quickly. I'll see you on Monday. Thank you." He put out his hand and I shook it. As they left I realised that perhaps I was beginning to receive the care I had been seeking. I of course still had a lot to learn about what a consultant said in comparison to what he did. I also realised that I hadn't asked him what he thought was actually wrong with me and he hadn't seemed awfully keen on telling me. I felt a little anxious as a result.

As I again absorbed myself with the predicaments of the NHS Barry wandered down the ward. He looked very ill. As a result of his condition he had lost about 40 Kilos over the space of 6 months and his sallow skin hung from his body in the same way as the dreadful pictures of the survivors from the Nazi concentration camps. He was a tall man and so at 6' 2" his condition emphasised how thin he had become. His stick like arms and tiny waist, which would barely hold up any of his clothes, emphasised the image. His complexion signalled his fatigue and as I watched him walk along the ward, it was clear by both his laboured movement and from his difficult breathing, that every step was an effort. He saw me look up, acknowledged me and came over and sat next to my bed. "Hi Edward, how are you doing?" "I'm ok Barry, thanks; you look to be struggling a bit! Are you ok?" He looked at the floor and took a deep breath. "No, not really!" As the next quarter of an hour passed by Barry explained how he had become ill. He had been a qualified draftsman by trade but had fallen so ill some 8 months ago that he hadn't worked since. Just before that his marriage had failed and he had been left at home on his own. When he fell ill the doctor's began various exploratory examinations and they eventually diagnosed possible Crohn's. I noticed he had a colostomy bag and I asked him why. The last exploratory examination he had undergone had involved a 'camera capsule' which was to film its passage through his system to identify the exact development of the disease within his digestive system. On the way through it had become stuck in a stricture in his small bowel. They had to conduct an emergency operation to remove it and found upon opening him up that he had an infection which would not allow them to complete the operation. Since he had first fallen ill he had lost weight at an alarming rate but once his bowel had been operated upon his weight loss accelerated rapidly. That had been several months ago and he was still waiting to receive corrective treatment. He had been told yesterday that it may be another 6 months before they could fit in an operation to try to reconnect his bowel. If he had undergone more clinical non invasive exploration by barium X ray or MRI they would have picked up on the strictures and never had to put the camera through him. He was frustrated by the bad decisions the medical staff had made and the resultant impact he now suffered. Tears filled his eyes and he fought to prevent them from rolling down his face. He told me how scared he was at how long he might have to wait for remedial surgery. He dabbed his eyes and for a brief moment sat silently looking at the floor wondering whether to continue. I didn't know where to look or what to say. I felt deeply sorry for him. I already understood how frightening it was to have to put your trust in the system having experienced the last few days. To translate this into months seemed incomprehensible. His life had altered so dramatically since he had fallen ill. From living a normal happy and busy life, he now experienced an institutionalised, boring, dependent, painful and worrying existence which was reliant upon the NHS. His diet was extreme, made up of a liquid supplement fed by a tube into his stomach. He was on extreme salt rations and was fed large meals which included a lot of fats and sugars as his metabolism was so ineffective at absorbing nutrients. Despite the extreme diets he continued to lose weight and constantly felt exhausted. He often became depressed as he felt so out of control. Only that morning he had been visited by an in house counsellor. She had tried to gauge his mood and in doing so questioned why he felt so down.

As he looked out of the window next to his bed, which he considered as his only escapism from his tawdry and miserable existence, he explained that he was struggling to cope with the concept of being dependent upon the hospital for the next 6 months and that he may never recover to be well enough to enjoy anything near a normal life. She had told him to stop dwelling on it and to expect to be well within weeks and that everyone would be doing everything within their power to enable his full recovery. As he put it, what a load of crap! As I listened I felt very angry that anyone should have to suffer like Barry. Eventually when he stopped talking he looked at me. During the whole conversation he had sat in the chair next to me looking towards the floor with his head bowed. He now stared me in the eye. "Make sure it doesn't happen to you!" I nearly croaked. Instead I put out my hand and held his in a hand shake of support. A forced smile started at the edge of his mouth, and with a small nod of his head he stood up. "We'll talk again some time." He shuffled off for a walk up the passageway outside the ward. I couldn't comprehend being dependent upon the care of the NHS for another 6 months. As I watched him depart a light went on in my brain. Con 2 had mentioned to me about having a camera capsule. I had just changed my mind. I didn't want it.

Lunch arrived with the announcement that my pre requested meal had been cancelled in favour of a colonoscopy diet. My small bland white bread turkey sandwich with Jelly to finish was nonetheless devoured. It felt great to be hungry again.

Once I had consumed my lunch, which took approximately 2 minutes, I returned to the papers. An occasional visit from a member of the nursing staff to check my observations and an impromptu visit from Doc 7, who appeared to have no clear role other than to ask me the usual twenty questions, interrupted me long enough to prevent me finishing another story. Despite running out of time to finish my broadsheets and tabloids, I was, as the afternoon wore on, really looking forward to seeing who came to see me. Visiting hours were becoming an anticipated highlight to the day.

It turned out to be like a party. My godmother Ro, followed by Ann, a friend of my Mums who was passing, Anthony, Tony and Emma, Ian and Sam , my godson, and Rachel who I had met only on New Year's Eve all turned up to see how I was doing that afternoon and evening. It was a constant flow of people and it delivered an enormous boost to my confidence and happiness. At the same time I could hear in the back of my mind the story Barry had told me about his once a fortnight visit that he received and so an occasional pang of guilt would subdue the fun I was having. Nonetheless at one point as evening descended and the visiting time was coming to a close a group of us had such hysterics that it sounded like there was a riot in our bay rather than a hospital sick bed. Even a colonoscopy supper couldn't dent my appreciation. It was fantastic to hear laughter. Tony, Emma and Rachel had been sat round for about an hour and we had been catching up on various stories, when a crescendo of bodily functional noise echoed around the ward like a symphony. From one bed, a cough, from another a belch, unbelievably a loud fart from two down and next door behind the curtain poor Harold contributed with a sleepy moan. The timing was exquisite. It was as if a conductor was stood on a platform in the middle of the ward bringing them all in on time. We all just looked at each other and cracked up. It was the sort of laughter that hurt. You tried desperately to keep it in and to laugh quietly but the more you looked at each other, the more it rolled on and on, until our composure was absolutely abandoned. Every time each of us looked up we set off again. Tears started to roll down our faces and our muffled laughter filled the ward. By the time they left we could have written a sketch show on the material we had generated.

Once they had gone and I lay peacefully, running their visit back through my mind it dawned on me how valuable the human spirit was in the face of adversity. If all you ever saw were the pompous consultants chasing their targets, the ineffective doctors wasting your time, the annoying newspaper collectors questioning your freedom of choice and the rude dieticians lacking any respect, the system could take away the very point of life itself. Without experiencing the absolute joy of talking to family and friends it would be very difficult to remain positive in this daunting environment. You wouldn't actually need to be ill as a perfectly fit person could be undermined just by the way they were treated as a human being in this place.

As night encroached a new team of staff that I hadn't seen before came on to start their shift. Bed time drinks were wheeled around the wards and dispensed to those who asked for them. It seemed a long time until Monday and whilst I was unaware of what a 'weekend in' meant, I wasn't looking forward to it. I had heard an occasional moan from staff about doing nights and doing weekend shifts but I didn't understand apart from the imposition on one's social life what their issues were. I was about to learn.

Sleep.

The previous shift had scuttled off like rats deserting a sinking ship. They had disappeared for their weekend at home in such a flourish that none of us had noticed their departure, particularly me as I had been so spoilt by the attention from my visitors. The first time it registered that there had been any change at all was the arrival of bedtime drinks and the realisation that some brand new faces were walking up and down the aisles of the ward. Not only were they new, it was also clear that there were far less of them. It was apparent that the shift was made up of some different and interesting characters. We now had a male nurse looking after us who wouldn't have looked out of place in the front row of a rugby league team. Graham, walked with a slight limp and his gruff voice hid a more gentle nature. Accompanying Graham was a nurse with about as much bedside manner as a character from Catherine Tait. I expected her to say, "Talking to me? Am I bothered?" at almost any point. Another more friendly nurse made up the team. She popped her head around most patients' curtains, "You ok luv?" It at least reflected an interest. They all spent a while readjusting to their task in hand and figuring out what faced them. I didn't get the impression that shift handover involved high degrees of communication or patient's notes. No one seemed to have explained to them the issue which may exist with each patient's condition. It appeared that in a similar fashion to an agric. student turning up at a lambing shed for the night shift you had to walk round and see what was going on to figure out what your next task would be. It all seemed bloody disorganised to me. You could tell by the occasional overheard comments between them that they were sizing up the task ahead and determining their allocation of responsibility between them. I originally assumed they were in charge of our ward alone but as the evening developed it became clear that they were in fact overseeing several wards. It suddenly dawned on me that this was a skeleton crew.

Earlier I had heard a patient being wheeled in to an isolation room opposite our ward. I had walked past the isolation room door, which was of course open, on the way to the bathroom and noticed an elderly lady in her 80's lying still, gaunt, pale faced and very asleep. I thought I had heard the elderly lady in the isolation room once before, but now it was clearer and more concerning," Help me; Please help me, someone, please." It was a plea of desperation in a voice that cut your heart strings. The 'please' was drawn out and beseeching and sounded like 'pleeease'. It became ever more eerie as no one attended to her and every 10 to 15 minutes she would try again to attract some attention. I assumed that she genuinely wanted something. I feared that incontinence or dementia were the likely culprits for her frightened and wanting state. For her and all of the patients within ear shot it was an uncomfortable experience. "Please help me. Please. Is there anyone there? Pleeease." I couldn't understand why the staff wouldn't attend to her. Occasionally a bell would sound at the nurse's station indicating that another patient needed some attention on one of the wards. It sounded for half an hour before someone finally reset it and hopefully attended the enquiry.

Our lights still remained on as midnight passed. None of us apart from Harold who muttered and moaned now on a regular basis could get to sleep. Harold had started making the moaning noises during visiting hours but since 9 O'clock he had become more unsettled. He made the sort of noise children make when they pretended to be a ghost. "Ooohh, Aaagh." It sounded frail and hollow. It was impossible to tell whether he was in pain or asleep and just dreaming as he never uttered anything except, "Ooohh, Aaagh" every few minutes. I couldn't understand why we were not being allowed to switch the lights off until at about half past midnight two of the nurses, one being Graham, came in to the ward with a trolley carrying various bits of equipment. They headed towards Barry s bed and began pulling the curtain around. It was clear from the noises that various procedures were being done involving taking blood samples, changing colostomy bags, cleaning Barry up and sorting out pump feeds and other various operations. It went on for half an hour. Arthur was on a drip with a pump which perpetually droned as had mine when I had received my transfusion. However this pump intermittently became faulty and would emit a high pitched bleep to indicate its failure. It was as irritating as finger nails drawn down a blackboard. Even so no one rushed to reset or repair it. Once in a while if someone was passing Arthur's bed they would duck in to his bay and reset it. Within a few minutes it would it would set off again stating a fault.

There was generally a lot of ward noise. A male ward is never the most pleasant experience. As had happened on countless other occasions the bodily noises of men; farting, coughing, clearing their throats, snorting, snoring and talking in their sleep all acted as a deterrent to your own rest. Tonight seemed to be a crescendo of such activity. In combination with bright lights, ongoing nursing tasks and the noises of people in discomfort both in and out of the ward, the male patient's bodily clatter and blasts were enough to prevent even a battle hardened veteran from sleeping. It was with some relief for all of us that finally our lights were switched off just after 1.00 am. Even so the staff hadn't finished. There appeared to be two beds which had been fouled and needed changing. This involved all three of the nurses to move the patients around as they remade the beds and cleaned up the patients where they lay. An unenviable task!

I kept looking at my watch. 1.00am became 2.00am. The elderly lady sporadically called out, "Please help me, someone, please help me. Why won't you help me? Please?" At the same time Dave unfortunately began to snore loudly. The pump connected to Arthur failed again and sent out its high pitched alarm. Harold continued to moan and unfortunately he began to smell too. Something had escaped his body. I could hear Barry listening to his TV on his headphones as he had also clearly given up on sleep. The nursing staff were now occupied elsewhere as a bell had been signalling at the nurse's station for nearly half an hour. I threw off a few more covers. The temperature on the ward had been rising all night and now I was uncomfortably hot. Somewhere a thermostat wasn't set correctly. I had really enjoyed my afternoon and evening of visitors but it had been tiring. Now I was beginning to feel exhausted again since sleep escaped me and yet still unable to nod off as the sounds around me never let up.

At about 2.30am a nurse arrived pushing a patient in a chair. She trundled him along the ward to the bed left unoccupied by the patient hunt initiated by Con I the previous day. It took her little time to settle him in. I wondered how he felt coming into such a noisy and unpleasant environment. I still couldn't sleep, so I guessed he had little chance.

I decided to join with Barry's way of thinking and fitted the headphones on and started to watch the TV. There was nothing on of any value, but it cut out the reality of the situation sufficiently to allow your mental well being to fall back towards some degree of equilibrium. I hoped in time it would lull me into some sort of sleep. It hadn't by 3.00am.

The first time I realised I had managed to drop off was when the lights were switched back on at 6.30 am. I was shattered. At some point my credit had run out on the TV which now showed a blank screen. I felt very cold as the heating which had raged in the early hours now seemed to be turned off, so I pulled a blanket back over me. From my first experience of this ward when everyone had said 'hello' upon my arrival which seemed so positive, my opinion of it and the whole ward concept had dropped alarmingly. Moral seemed to have dropped too. My fellow patients appeared tired and sullen. I couldn't see how treating patients in the manner we were all treated during the night, could be beneficial to our health in any way at all? Sleep and rest is one of the most important aspects of recovery and care and yet the experience we had all endured one way or another within the last 8 hours would not be out of place in an interrogation programme. I had as a result of our most recent experience become ever more disillusioned with the NHS system. As I looked around the ward at the exhausted faces of the other patients sharing my plight I could tell I wasn't the only one thinking about it.

A nurse wandered down to the far end of the ward to see how the newest intern was doing. It appeared that Mr Fraser hadn't got on that well either. "You sleep ok, love?" she asked. "No I didn't. I've sat in this chair all night" answered Mr Fraser. "No you haven't love, you would have been in bed; I'm sure. Didn't you get put to bed when you came in?" Mr Fraser started to sound a bit cross, "No I've been sat in this chair all night. I couldn't sleep. No one could sleep in here. It was terrible." I was so pleased it wasn't just me. The concerning aspect of their conversation however was the complete lack of appreciation from the nurse as to what the conditions were like on the ward and how difficult it was to sleep. She appeared completely unaware of the problems and seemed mostly apathetic towards our plight.

It was clear that Harold had indeed had an accident in the night. The odour was becoming stronger now. The night shift who had apparently been busy elsewhere all night, never bothered with it. It wasn't until Rosie and part of her new weekend team came on that anything was done for him. It turned out that he had fouled the bed and that his catheter had become detached. Poor Harold had laid in his own mess from sometime in the early hours. As the nursing staff cleaned him up and changed his bed he moaned louder than ever. By all accounts he now had some bed sores. I wasn't surprised. I was however appalled at the lack of respect and care he had received. Harold was probably in his mid eighties. He had no doubt led as important a life as any of us. He now lay in a hospital bed totally dependent upon the hospital staff for his well being. He would have at some point elected to put his trust in someone to take care of him as he fell ill. Whether it was his judgement, or that of a relative it wouldn't have been given lightly. In this day and age you do expect a minimum standard of care which is going to at least meet a level retaining a degree of self respect. You don't expect to have to lie in your own excrement or be treated as a child just because you have temporarily lost a degree of self control.

Respect was lacking in other areas of his care with just as much abandon. When nursing staff had to undertake the responsibility for feeding Harold they showed such a degree of disdain that they were verging on derision. I anticipated the senior nursing staff leading by example and speaking to him with respect. "Mr Roberts would you like some breakfast? Mr Roberts, you need to eat your porridge. Would you like some more porridge? Is there anything I can get you Mr Roberts? Let me help you, here you are! Well done Mr Roberts, this will make you feel better," would have been adequate, encouraging and supportive with a degree of respect well suited to a man in his eighties. However "Haaarold, come on lovey, now you know you've got to try some more, come on Haaarrold." The elongated vowels, in a dressed up 'Steptoe and son' version emphasised the indignation he suffered at their hands. It was as if he was 2 or 3 years old and hadn't quite mastered feeding himself, not over 80 and lying in a bed fallen ill and incapable of looking after himself. 'Good lad', 'that's my boy' and 'aren't you clever' are barely the terms of reference one expects in one's senior years. Often the nurses openly discussed his eating habits as though none of us could hear a word they said, "He's not going to eat that; There's no point in trying; We're wasting our time." Nor was this lack of care in isolation. Over the next few nights and particularly over the weekend Harold's incontinence was regular and ever less well observed. Although on one occasion the nurses were aware within a short time that he needed some attention, more often than not it was hours after the event that someone would finally even recognise that he needed their care. Each night over the weekend, Friday to Sunday inclusive, he messed his bed. On each night he lay in either urine which had escaped his catheter or faeces which escaped his body. He lay in it for a long time, from about 2.00am through until 6.30am. His catheter often leaked and they irregularly emptied his bag. It was only on the day shifts that it was noticed more regularly simply by a greater abundance of staff activity and a more qualified and responsible person being present. The night shift was considerably less careful. For instance an open bucket would be carried in to empty the contents of Harold's catheter bag. Graham would plonk the bucket down between my bed and Harold's. He would then unplug the bag and drain it into the bucket. I could see the fluid and smell the ammonia as we all listened to the sound of the fluid filling the bucket. It wasn't pleasant. Harold's breathing was occasionally so bad that they would put him on a nebuliser. At its worst his breath sounded as raspy as the noise produced by standing on frosted bracken. It rattled and crackled as fluid on his lungs tried to prevent his breathing working effectively. I wondered what sort of life he had led. What had Harold's life included? What had he achieved? Where were his friends and family? I knew for sure that whatever the answers were to those questions he would never have expected to find himself in this dreadful position. Nor did he deserve to. No one did. Whether it was Harold or the poor lady in the isolation room across the passage they all deserved better care. Elderly people should receive a recognised minimum standard of care which should be fundamental to any health service. The nurses and carers should provide the elderly with a dignified and respectful end to their lives. It is no less important than another extremely important aspect of health care, paediatrics. Yet paediatric departments are so often the best in any hospital. They tend to have better facilities, better staff and a much better focus on the job in hand. No one would argue for a change in the importance of a good paediatric department. I find it difficult to understand why life's end is any less important than life's beginning.

On the Sunday night I was blocked from sleep as a result of the noise on the ward. A combination of other people sleep talking, the cries of the lady in the isolation room, "Pleeeease help me, please" and the bleeps of associated drips and pumps stopped me from sleeping. It was 2.30am and I decided to nip to the loo. I went out in to the brightly lit corridor. One of the lights was flashing in the nurse's station with its associated bleeping sound. No one was there. I looked up and down the corridor. It was like a ghost town. I wondered where they could all be. I decided that it would be a valuable experience to see whether anyone was about at all. I set off up the corridor. I walked past ward after ward, filled with sleeping patients making similar noises to my own ward. I went past several nurse's stations with no one in attendance. After maybe 5 or 6 wards and about 70 yards I turned around and set off back. On reaching my own ward I went the other way as far as I could go. Again, there was not a member of staff to be seen. I headed back and went to the loo. When I came out I stood with amazement in the corridor. I had been 15 minutes at least now patrolling the corridor and there was still no evidence of any staff. Anything could be happening right now, a patient dying, a security issue, a fire and the night shift would be oblivious. The elderly lady lay prostrate in her bed and called out every few minutes. "Help me please, why won't anyone help me. Plee-eease help me." I quickly looked in to her room, but daren't go any further. I neither wanted to confuse her or frighten her. Nonetheless it was heartbreaking to feel so useless in not being able to administer some degree of comfort to her. The problem was that there was no one to help her, and even if there was they would probably ignore her anyway. The thought of my grandfather lying here many years ago, scared, alone and dependent upon sub standard care suddenly pierced my soul. I was utterly aghast and ashamed as a human being at the lack of care that was being shown to these people. Out of all of the times it crossed my mind, this was the one time when I was seriously close to doing a runner. I had no confidence in the hospital or the people looking after me. I didn't feel safe. Only the thought of having my colonoscopy kept me there. I so desperately wanted to find out what was the matter with me. I walked back in to my ward and quietly sat back on to my bed. The noise in the ward was the same so I slipped my TV headphones on and let the garbage on early morning TV drain over me. I was still awake an half an hour later when I heard Graham turn up at the nurse's station. We had been without nursing cover along our corridor where probably 50 patients resided for an hour.

I still cannot understand why budgets, targets, protocols, initiatives and political buzz words are all held in a higher regard than patient's care and Harold's life. It should never get to the point that politicians are allowed to discuss budgets running into billions of pounds and new concepts or projects costing millions when a man cannot be cleaned up within a few minutes of being ill, a woman cannot be seen after calling out repeatedly, a pump cannot be replaced when it's faulty and a nurse's bell cannot be answered in seconds never mind minutes or hours. Patients should never be left for any length of time unobserved and unsupervised. It is all too apparent that there is a chasm of misunderstanding which is so enormous between the reality on the ground in a ward and the image perceived by the distant trust managers in their offices or the politicians with their notional ideas sat on their benches in chambers.

I realised in the moment when I stood alone in the corridor that in everything I had experienced so far, that the one common denominator in all of the failings of the NHS system, was a lack of clear focus for the purpose of the existence of the service itself; the patient. It was as sobering an instant in my life as I could remember for some time despite all of my recent upheaval. The scale of the problem facing such an enormous organisation suddenly seemed extremely frightening, not just for me, but for everyone reliant upon our health service. It was a frightening enough experience to be genuinely scared for your own well being whilst you were trapped under its control. It was a frightening enough experience to seriously consider running away.

On that Saturday morning I drifted back to watching the nursing staff busying themselves around the ward. There was such diversity in the quality of the people. There were wonderful dedicated nurses at one end of the scale and totally incompetent managers at the other and everything in between. What a mess! I wished Rosie would come and ask me again what I thought about the NHS again. I had a few things to say.

Once the nursing team had cleared up the work remaining from the night shift, they started dealing with their daily tasks. It wasn't long before my blood pressure and other vital signs had been checked and logged on to my charts. I needed to provide some additional embarrassing information about my bowel activity to go on to my record sheet. It wasn't the best time to talk about it at a mealtime. Nonetheless breakfast came around much the same as the day before and with an equivalent amount of time spent by the nurses administering sugar and milk.

Fortunately however for me, it appeared to be the 'paper collecting' lady's day off. I still had an article to finish about the financial mismanagement of the NHS.

Super Bug.

Although my health had improved significantly I was still bleeding. The trips to the bathroom indicated that there was still a slow bleed somewhere. I hoped that it was gradually healing. The ugly and foul Melina was still dark but less regular. I still had to use the bits of cardboard, cover them with paper and instruct a nurse that I had left a sample. It seemed irrelevant if the consultants and doctors never viewed it. It also seemed downright unsanitary. Fortunately my other symptoms had now withdrawn to just general soreness, low energy reserves and a feeling of utter exhaustion which I decided was caused by the lack of sleep as much as anything else. As I was so tired and since the colonoscopy meals were far from nourishing I hadn't yet leapt out of bed for my morning ablutions. It was after 10 am before I decided to venture forth.

As I showered and tried to improve my overall demeanour, I noticed various concerning inadequacies within the facilities that hadn't been apparent before. The cord which acted as the switch for the shower was now held together by a grimy plaster. The bin which was provided to dispense with used paper hand towels was full and overflowing. The floor looked a little grubbier than usual. The lavatory was short of toilet roll and looked slightly worse for wear. The hand soap dispenser had run dry. On top of all of that someone else had clearly used the bathroom that morning. They clearly hadn't shown too much care about the state they had left it in as sediment from their occupation was settled in the base of the shower. I peered around the facilities expecting a large grimy cockroach to run up a wall as it felt like I was in a facility in a third world country rather than the UK. I realised that the facilities had neither been inspected nor cleaned that morning. It appeared that weekend cover for cleaners was outside the hospital budget.

As I made my way back to the ward I quickly looked in to the other lavatories and bathrooms as well. I'm sure that anyone overlooking my clandestine investigations would have wondered what on earth I was doing as 'Bodie and Doyle' style I poked the doors open with my toe and peered in to the facilities. There was evidence of a similar lack of attention there too. The last time I had seen a cleaner had been yesterday morning on the ward. There had in fact been a considerable amount of dialogue between a sister and one of the cleaners as to the ability of other various cleaning staff only a few feet from my bed. . It seemed that she had found missed bits during her patrol. I pondered on just how difficult it was to keep a facility like this clean. My synopsis was that it was actually quite tricky. The hospital hadn't exactly been built with cleaning in mind. There were so many nooks and crannies and so much variation in surfaces, rooms, equipment and features. The basics such as sanitary supply equipment was simple enough; keep it stocked up. But the actual cleaning needed a degree of imagination and a mindset which fought infection, was determined and fastidious and took pride in a relatively menial task despite the degree of importance forced upon it. Finding the right people to deal with it was a problem but finding enough people who wanted to do it properly all of the time was always going to be a big issue. Our society has over the last twenty years developed a pecking order which has lent a materialistic playground mentality towards the comparative values of the jobs we perform and the money we earn from our particular vocations. Being a cleaner in an NHS hospital wasn't going to be the top of most people's want lists. In today's economy most of these tasks were being performed by immigrant eastern european labour employed by large contracting firms who believed it was a step on the bottom rung of the ladder. Their contribution to society was about what they might get out of it rather than what they might contribute. I continued pondering.

Once back in the ward I stowed my wash things and lay on the bed. As I rested I looked through the now enormous array of reading material I possessed, brought to me by my various visitors. I spotted an article on MRSA. As I read the newspaper I discovered a story about an 18 year old TA soldier who had died from PVI MRSA as a result of a scratch he had acquired from a gorse bush. His subsequent shower in facilities harbouring the deadly agent killed him within 24 hours. It was a shocking story. I sat up and looked around my environment. If it could kill a fit and strong young man in 24 hours we were all potentially dead meat in here. Within the last few months I was led to understand that this hospital had itself experienced two superbug outbreaks which had resulted in both mortality and ward closures. I pulled the covers a little closer in a pathetic attempt to defend myself and I eyed the plastic cup on my bedside table with suspicion. I thought about every cough and sneeze within the ward over the last few days and just how many of the surfaces had been touched by all and sundry. I looked across at Dave suffering from pneumonia. He must be a real target for the disease. I studied the dried blood on my canulas on the back of both hands and wondered whether the dressings acted as any barrier at all to the disease. I thought about all of the blood and the sores, the surgical injuries and the inserted needles within this ward alone within the last few days. I suddenly remembered just how many blood samples had been taken from my arms in various places. One had to accept that they were all considerably more invasive and more serious than a bit of gorse. Gorse was very nasty stuff and left some pretty nasty scratches if you ploughed straight through it, however compared to someone taking blood sample after blood sample and leaving dried blood on your arms it fell in to a far less serious arena for developing an environment for an attacking super bug. I was living in a risk assessor's worst nightmare and suddenly a bloody worrying place to be.

I thought back to the conversation between the cleaner and the sister. The problem at the time was related to unclean surfaces that had been spotted during normal nursing activity. It was apparent that some floor areas hadn't been wiped where tables and trolleys stood in the way. Instead they had been cleaned around. There had also been some misses on the curtain rails too, as well as the window ledges and even some of the bedside tables which were overflowing with contents. It was fascinating that despite the unclean surfaces being apparent no one had yet bothered to do anything about it. Nurses didn't clean just as cleaners didn't nurse, thankfully. Considering the risks at stake one would have assumed that even if nurses weren't allowed or prepared to do a bit of wiping down they would have called in the cleaning staff or the contractors immediately to rectify the situation. I looked at my bay with concern. The two of them continued their animated discussion in the middle of the ward which concluded that one of the other cleaners wasn't up to the mark. The cleaner who found herself having to defend her department's lack of quality work was guarded about her own contribution; "It must be that girl on the other shift. I always move them trolleys and such like. Having said that it's not ever so easy to reach sometimes." As they left the ward I could hear her repeatedly confirming it wasn't her and that she was doing a good job, it was that other girl, 'lazy cow'. It was clear that the bugs were considerably brighter than the management and the staff.

Another conversation I was party to over the weekend concerned me even more. On the night shift the nurses had been transporting full bed pans from one ward facility to the next to dispose of the contents. There had been a problem with the disposal facilities on the ward in question. Staff had been walking about the hospital corridors with full bed pans sometimes dripping on the corridor floors. The story had leaked out as easily as the transported fluids and had been discussed by a couple of the nurses on the day shift at the nurse's station. There was going to be 'hell to pay' but that didn't really instil anymore confidence in my state of mind as a result of knowing that it had happened.

I hunted through my stack of journalism to see whether there were any more interesting stories to read and came across a very relevant report detailing the results of a recent British Medical Journal survey. The survey concluded that the single biggest milestone in the improvement of the nation's health within the last one and a half centuries was sanitation. This survey put sanitation forward as a more significant contributor to the overall improvement of health than vaccines, antibiotics and anaesthesia. It discussed the particular contribution of two men who made a significant impact over 150 years ago.

In Britain, the first modern cholera epidemic occurred in 1831-32, causing over 23,000 deaths. This epidemic did not produce an immediate burst in public health legislation from the British government, but it did have the lasting effect of launching the sanitary reform movement. The movement was led by Edwin Chadwick, a Minister of Parliament, and several other ardent students and friends of philosopher Jeremy Bentham, whose utilitarianism had taught them that the task of government was to provide the greatest good for the greatest number of citizens. Charged in 1839 with the surveying of the sanitary conditions among the poor and working classes, Chadwick and colleagues produced in 1842 an exhaustive and influential tome; The Report on the Sanitary Condition of the Labouring Population of Great Britain. Spurred on by this and other reports, the sanitary reform movement prospered and appealed to public opinion of the day. A Public Health Bill and a Nuisances Removal Bill (known unofficially as the Cholera Bill) were ultimately passed in 1848, but only because the arguments of the reformers were amplified by the footsteps of another cholera pandemic approaching from the continent.

Two more British epidemics in 1848 and 1849 brought at least 250,000 cases and 53,000 deaths. It was during these scourges that John Snow began his investigations of cholera.

By 1848 Edwin Chadwick had become the Sanitary Commissioner of London, and was very influential in the city's approach towards cholera. He believed that filth in rivers was less dangerous than filth in sewers. As Commissioner, he had the power to have sewers regularly flushed into the River Thames. Contrary to Dr. John Snow, he was a strong believer in the theory that epidemics were generated spontaneously from dirt, and that basic sanitation rather than specific avoidance of cholera germs would control the disease. He rejected with scorn as mere hypothesis Snow's germ theory, as described in Snow's 1855 book. While others had come to accept the germ theory, Chadwick remained a committed sanitarian to the end, telling a newspaper reporter shortly before his death in 1890: "I cannot tell you how strongly I believe in soap and water as a preventive of epidemics" (Weekly Dispatch, July 13, 1890). At the time Chadwick knew very little about the impact that such a simple decision would have upon the nation's health. It just seemed a good idea.

John Snow (1813-1858) was a leading British anesthesiologist who volunteered for several years to conduct his own investigations of the mode of cholera transmission. Snow is best known for his investigations and intervention during a bad outbreak of cholera that began on August 31, 1854 in the Broad Street, Golden Square section of London. In a nutshell, Snow observed that the cases of cholera were predominantly among people who had drunk water from a pump on Broad Street. Snow asked for the pump handle to be removed, and the outbreak - which had already begun to decline due to a fleeing populace and the deaths of many in the neighborhood - was terminated.

As I read the articles and learnt about the historical development of modern health and sanitation it became crystal clear that the people in charge of our present day health service had forgotten some of the most fundamental aspects to health management. The alarming similarity between Victorian basic health issues and the problems facing the NHS with MRSA seemed almost too obvious to compare. Yet fundamentally the solution to preventing contamination and the spread of disease was simple. Keep the place clean, keep the patients and the staff clean, keep wounds well dressed and keep people apart so that they are less likely to spread the disease. Finally monitor the level of the disease within the environment, the people and the hospital equipment by conducting regular swab tests and analysis.

Let's face it MRSA and other super bugs are always going to be a serious issue in hospitals. Over 1000 patients a year are struck down by clostridium dificile whilst in hospital in the UK at present. This is an incredibly serious problem and a terrifying experience for anyone in hospital. Patients harbour MRSA on their skin or up their nose without harm to themselves. However, these patients may develop infections if the MRSA spread to other parts of their body such as from their colonised nose to a wound. Some patients have a particularly increased risk of developing an infection. I fell in to the category only too neatly. Patients at greatest risk include those with breaks in their skin due to wounds or indwelling catheters or canulas which allow MRSA to enter the body, and those with certain types of deficiency in their immune system, such as low numbers of white cells in their blood.

I was nervous as hell all of a sudden. I was a high risk case. I had experienced a blood transfusion, my haemoglobin level was low, my immune system was weak, I had two bloody cannulas in my hands which looked a mess under the dressings and I was surrounded by ill people. On top of that there was evidence that the cleaning standards within the ward were below par. I never saw the nurses observing hygiene religiously, they were only wearing gloves when they were dealing with something nasty and they never used the hand cleansers above each patient's bed. The risks from cross infection and contaminated equipment were in even a layman's opinion sufficiently high enough to expect someone with a degree of authority in the management of the hospital and particularly with the recent poor track record to at least notice the possibilities. I pulled the sheets up even higher in a pathetic attempt to make myself feel a little more secure and defend myself better from the potential squadrons of bugs.

One thing which frustrated me intently was the ward system. It lent itself to the spread of disease. I was so close to Harold that some of the time I could smell him. Only a partly drawn curtain existed between us and that was only some of the time. I couldn't understand why the architects and planners for the department of health didn't more strongly advocate the concept of single rooms or at least isolation sheets as used in Dutch hospitals. I just could not understand why the nursing staff failed to use the hand cleaners and how infrequently they used gloves and other protective clothing when treating patients although some did occasionally. I suspected that almost all of the nursing staff went home in their uniforms and came back from their domestic duties the next day carrying all sorts of bacteria on them. I still kept thinking back to my original diagnosis of dysentery and how little priority appeared to be shown to the environment within which I was held.

This wasn't about some elitist private/privacy issue. I was already tired of people in the system defending the NHS as being the common man's approach to health care. I found their simplistic defence about it being more ethically correct than the snobby private system with their 'fancy' beds and equipment so childlike that it was inadmissible. I could sense opinion being thrust at me by consultants, nurses and cleaning staff all of the time defending their 'precious' health service. It was as if they lived so closely to it that they couldn't see that the patients in it, who actually paid for it, should be allowed some degree of input into what it looked like. I sat and thought about the issues with ever greater concentration. My brain had become octane fuelled through ensuing fear, a growing sense of frustration and anger at this ridiculous situation. I could feel the adrenalin coursing through my veins as I became more strident in my thought processes. I imagined that the first argument thrown at me would be about the capital required to build hospitals with single rooms. Building hospitals which were about patient well being were going to cost more money. Hospitals with separate patient facilities were clearly going to cost a lot more money; or were they? An article in one of the papers stated that the operational costs of running a hospital exceeded the capital costs within two years of running the hospital from a standing start. If a hospital was going to be there for maybe a hundred years or even only fifty what was spent on the infrastructure in the first place was a small hill of beans in comparison to how much it would cost to run. Even I, a simple farmer, could see the ongoing possibilities for saving money as a result of improved care. I thought about how many times I had been moved within the last 6 days. Surely moving patients about was a bad idea. I had no figures to hand bit in my mind I supposed that there must be a heavy correlation between cross infection, clinical errors and patient movement. I found Con1's patient movement request even more bizarre as I considered this point. If patients coming in to a hospital either through A&E or through referral from a GP were allocated a single room on a ward appropriate to their condition from the outset they were bound to be more secure, more relaxed and more likely to improve their recovery time. Admittedly admission wards were an essential requirement, but since at this point of a patient's journey through the system, diagnosis was incomplete, it seemed lunacy to put them all on a ward together. If at no other stage in their hospitalization, at the point of admission, isolation should be a foregone conclusion in the management of patient care and the minimisation of the risk of disease outbreaks. "Healthcare must start to give more attention to the patient" I thought as I became more and more fired up, "Meeting targets must not be used as some sort of smokescreen excuse for sacrificing patient's dignities and human rights." I hoped none of the staff were looking at me as I would probably have bored holes through their heads with my burning eyes.

As I considered all of the concerns I had generated in relation to the hygiene of my immediate surroundings it made me angry to think of how much deployed resource went to waste. The very thought of Patricia Hewitt advocating massive budgetary spends on various new database technology and the £300 million additional annual cost of the 'Golden Contract' for the GP's angered me deeply. What the health service needed to do was to get the basics right first. Clean hospitals, new facilities, better training at all levels, more nurses, reinstatement of Matrons, accountability for the trusts management, league tables reflecting poor performance and policies implemented to make sure standards were met. It was no good having some political headline target about reducing waiting times if all it did was take away the focus from the important aspects of health care such as the well being of the patient whilst they were in care. Let's face it, a patient that is less tired, better fed, more relaxed, at less risk to secondary infection and receiving quicker treatment will recover faster and spend less time blocking a bed anyway. With the correct management in place the waiting time issue goes away on its own. I knew from my own recent experience that some of the people on my ward were waiting for tests or procedural examinations including myself. But because no one worked a weekend and consultants only worked on examinations on certain days and that the present systems in place created huge administrative trails which blocked up the system as well, a lot of patient's bed time is taken up just waiting. I know as a taxpayer I would be perfectly content to see another 1p in the pound spent on the health service as long as I was confident that the 1p was going towards meeting basic patient care improvements and not some jumped up Tony Blair 'bollocks' idea.

I remembered a comment made to me by one of my visitors regarding the Gerry Robinson TV programme on the NHS. Mr Robinson had concluded that he was left feeling incredibly frustrated that actually quite small sums of money properly and sensibly spent could have produced very large results in terms of reduced waiting lists. In his opinion however, very large sums of money had been thrown at the NHS and produced very little. He had determined that hospitals lacked a sense of management and that they had no real focus on quality, whether it was related to staff, services, conditions or standards. Having seen it firsthand I whole heartedly agreed with him.

As the weekend wore on my initial observations became more and more poignant. By the time Monday morning arrived the facilities that the patients depended upon resembled something out of a scene from a flight delayed Palma airport. In fact I would go further and compare them to facilities one would expect from an institution which had been under siege for a week. The lavatories were dirty and the floors particularly filthy. All of the soap dispensers had run out as had all of the paper towel holders. The floors were covered in hand towels as the bins had overflowed sometime on Saturday afternoon. It became obvious that a clandestine operation to pilfer the loo roll from the toilets on the other wards was going to be required by Sunday afternoon. It reminded me of the days back in time when all of the agricultural college student houses were stocked up from the facilities in college; but not quite so much fun.

We didn't see any cleaners over the weekend at all. As the rubbish bins were crammed full of waste produced by patients and visitors alike stacking began near to the bins. Within a few feet of my bed was the main rubbish bin for our ward. Every visitor and patient on the ward had at one time or another walked past the end of my bed and shoved their collection of food wrappers, bottles and various other refuse generated by their visits and activities in to this bin. Its lid now wouldn't close and the smell from it reflected a need for a large refuse lorry to arrive soon and dispose of its contents. Unable to bear the pong, which was slightly worse than Harold, I forced the piled up rubbish down in to the bin, shut the lid and went to wash my hands.

Because of the weekend there had been considerably more visitor traffic, which of course not only relied upon the same facilities as the patients but also brought in higher risks of contamination from outside the hospital. To be frank the place just looked dirty, uncared for and overlooked. It became a very disturbing experience using the bathroom facilities as it was very obvious that there was no hygiene management taking place. On one occasion I went to use the toilet. On the floor in a piece of cardboard lay a sample of someone else's excreta which had not been collected by nursing staff. I found a member of staff and asked them to remove it immediately. They did so but with an air of ordinary day to day activity and certainly not with any observational concern. As a result of the deplorable state of the patient's facilities by the end of the weekend I was not entirely surprised to see a whole team of cleaners arrive on Monday morning. They blitzed the entire facility within the space of an hour. By the time either doctors or consultants showed their faces there was no evidence of the mess we had all lived with in the preceding two days and nights. It was like a clandestine cover up. It was an appalling demonstration of where everyone's focus and priorities lay.

One cleaner on each ward for an hour on each day over the weekend would easily have maintained a minimum standard of hygiene. Even on an overtime rate I guessed the entire weekend would not run to more than a dozen cleaning staff costing £1000 and that was being pessimistic. Over a whole year £50,000 spent on weekend cleaning making sure that the facilities were kept up to scratch over essentially 28% of the time in the year seemed a small price to pay in ensuring a clean and safe environment for thousands of patients in a year. Someone somewhere wasn't looking at the bigger picture and it was time they did. Within only a few yards of where I lay there were dozens of elderly 'at risk' patients, many of whom were totally dependent upon nursing care. I found it disturbing to see how infrequently they received treatment or attention. They often lay in their own mess, their facilities were not cleaned properly, there were insufficient staff to respond to their calls or queries and there was no ongoing management of their environment in place over the weekends to protect their well being. It was categorically negligent.

MRSA; Clostridium difficile bacteria; Super bugs; hospital infections; whatever you wanted to call it, had an opportunity to strike under these conditions. I thought back to the debacle within the A & E department upon my admission and the staff eating fish and chips. Right at the beginning of my experience the 'shop window' sold to me the conditions that this hospital viewed as acceptable. Nonetheless I was finding it hard to accept that in 2007 the NHS had not managed to work out that a fundamental aspect of their job was the health and well being of the patient whilst under their management. I decided it was time someone looked after my well being sooner than later.

I called a nurse by pressing my bell. I hadn't done that for a long time. "Excuse me," I said as she arrived, "I'd like my dressings changed. I've got blood all over the back of my hands. When I shower or wash they get wet." It was a congealed mess under my dressings. "Do I actually need these things in anymore?" I asked. She looked at me with a degree of scepticism. It appeared I was not as urgent a case as another she had to attend to. She looked like she was about to head off. I stepped up the anti. "Can I have my canulas removed and my hands re dressed now please?" She saw I had the bit between my teeth, smiled sweetly and headed off to collect the necessary equipment. She arrived back in minutes and set about sorting out the smelly unsightly dressings. Once she had redressed my hands I casually asked her to see whether Harold was ok as I could smell something which didn't need a lot of imagination to work out what might be wrong. She went to look. Within a few minutes several nurses were working behind his curtain lifting him, cleaning him and remaking his bed around him. I felt incredibly sorry for Harold. It appeared that a bed sore had become worse. I was sure that patients with bed sores needed turning but didn't bother mentioning it as I assumed they all knew what they were doing. Oddly he never got turned.

An article on the Crimea attracted my attention and as I picked up the supplement to begin reading it I wondered how Florence Nightingale had got on with sanitation. I guessed she was a damned site better at it than this lot.

Food and new bedfellows.

Jamie Oliver and his school dinners often came to mind as I watched the catering staff wheeling in meal after meal of the most uninspiring bland nutritionally impaired slop. I, of course, usually found myself unable to take part in the full experience as I was either too ill to eat anything, on a specific procedural diet or 'nil by mouth.' On the odd occasion I was permitted to eat I was fed the outstanding 'Egon Ronay' colonoscopy diet. Over the weekend I was allowed two servings of jelly, one hardboiled egg, a bland turkey sandwich and some clear soup which was more like used bath water. In all, over two days I consumed less than 500 calories. My compatriots seemed to fair no better despite the fact that they had been given a degree of choice from a menu which offered little sustenance. In a continuing theme from breakfast, with each meal, staff approached every bed to serve either sugar and milk or custard and gravy. Despite whatever food had been ordered gravy and custard was offered from a jug reminiscent of something you would have experienced back at School in the 70's. It was usually accepted by the recipient in some attempt to mask the slop which was trying to pass as food on their plate. A couple of new guys, Pete and George, who had turned up over the weekend were particularly vocal as they never seemed to receive what they had ordered. Whether it was breakfast, lunch or tea at least once a day since their arrival into the hospital and throughout their movements from ward to ward, one or the other received someone

153

else's order. They had dutifully eaten whatever it was each time but then spent a while in earnest debate with each other or whoever was in earshot after the meal.

George was a big man in every sense. A born and bred mariner for all of his life, he showed the etiquette of one who lived as he wished and was never told to reconsider his habits. He was about 20 stone, aged mid forties, and suffered from acute diabetes as well as other secondary implications. His cherry red legs were exposed by his rather dirty and untidy shorts. His inability, due to the discomfort, of having anything over them including his bed clothes, left his ugly affliction on view to all. In keeping with his grim appearance his toe nails were of a grotesque length as he was unable to cut them due to the potential shock resulting from his condition. They were reminiscent of a caricature we all grew up with as children of vampires and witches. His breathing often became difficult resulting in his reliance upon a nebuliser and he was unsteady enough on his feet to need a walking frame to move about with. Nonetheless he had the heart of a lion and a voice which carried a country mile. Peter was a stereotypical local chap in his mid sixties. Lightly overweight, grey and sallow, he wore pyjamas Hyacinth Bouquet would have been proud. He usually snored, said little unless prompted and showed a general lack of regard for his compatriots in watching his television without headphones so that we all had to listen to whatever he watched. His grey mop was set off by an equivalent mass of hair protruding from ears and nostrils alike. He would often stare in to space with his mouth hung open in a gawp. However, once prompted and adequately stirred, Peter used the English language with gusto and a local accent which did nothing for interpretation. He was always wearing a big smile whenever his family visited him and he seemed a kind and normal soul. When he wasn't staring in to space, he occupied some of his time consuming crisps or other junk food that his visitors provided him with. He had a heart condition and was in hospital for an exploratory procedure which seemed to be taking forever to organise. I couldn't help but question the advice he was receiving on his lifestyle activities since he was suffering from a condition not helped by his intake. However in comparison, his other favourite bad habits which included diligent caving expeditions up his nostrils and musical composure from his rear orifice were less appealing.

On the plus side our new team mates were quite vocal in their criticism of the hospital generally and the catering in particular. I occasionally waded in with a few affirmatives but spent more time listening than talking. In fact within a few hours of their arrival the new faces complained so avidly that they had quite an impact upon the delivery of the catering service, as eventually a member of staff was sent up to the ward to enquire what issues they had with the food. George was indeed a vocal sort who liked his opinion to be voiced. George in particular said what we all thought and at a level which we could all hear. It was encouraging to see someone who was totally dependent upon the service being prepared to have a go. George was fearless and I was duly impressed. It met all of my 'shouting' criteria. As a group of patients we weren't that bad and I guessed there would have been a lot worse people to look after. It did make me wonder how the nursing staff found the inspiration to keep going in the face of adversity when they were presented with difficult people to look after. Rude, ignorant, uneducated, dangerous, non compliant or just plain stupid people who might try and undo the good which everyone had tried to apply to their recovery. I remembered a story recounted to me by a friend. He had been stuck in hospital and in the next bed was a man who had suffered from domestic violence which had resulted in a large proportion of his hand being severed. Surgeons had successfully reattached the hand but he was under strict instructions to not move as it would jeopardise the graft. He wouldn't stay in bed however as he constantly wanted to use the loo and whilst nurses did their best to make him use a bottle in the bed he always got up to go to the loo. Each time the movement risked the limb being rejected. After three trips to the loo the nurses followed him to find that he wasn't going to the loo at all but outside the hospital for a fag. You just can't help some people. I guess that being faced with that every day it would be easy to lose your inspiration for nursing.

Food aside, George was also prepared to sort out as much as possible himself. His ongoing reliance upon the health service seemed to have taught him that it was better to take matters into your own hands at times rather than wait for the staff to act. He believed in expressing his opinion at sufficient decibels that someone had to take notice. He became involved in considerable drama when one of our fellow ward members became suddenly ill and he was required to use his vocal capabilities to attract some nursing attention.

My previous partners in crime had been shifted out of the ward quite suddenly. Dave had been allowed home on the Saturday morning. No sooner had he escaped than Pete arrived to take his place. Arthur was wheeled away on to another ward the same day and George came in to replace him. Mr Fraser who had only been wheeled in on the Friday night was out by Sunday morning and replaced by someone I never did manage to meet. Poor Mr Fraser left as a result of his deteriorating condition as he suffered a mild heart attack on the ward on Sunday morning. He suddenly started making a lot of guttural noises and pressed his call bell. He cried out in pain so unexpectedly and with such a yelp that we all became very aware that something was seriously wrong. None of the nursing staff arrived to see to him however. Barry who was the nearest and George with legs, the colour of red grapes and sucking air like Edmund Hilary leapt off their beds and went across to see him. I could hear him explaining to them that he had a shooting pain down his arm and didn't feel too well. George, who despite having impaired mobility as a result of his condition, was half way up the ward stumbling and yet still looking for assistance for Mr Fraser. He bellowed out "Nurse, Nurse" before I could even get out of bed. A nurse who finally heard the commotion and George's persistent shouting arrived forthwith. George tried his best to explain what had happened but the exertion of attending to Mr Fraser had shortened his breath to such a degree that it prevented him from enlightening the nurse as she reached her failing patient. She called for additional assistance as it became clear George needed a nebuliser as a result of his efforts. Mr Fraser could be heard registering that he thought he had suffered a heart attack. The nurse's initial reaction was to say the least, extraordinary! Mr Fraser was clearly distressed and ill. George sat on the end of his bed and Barry stood nearby showing concern. Even Pete and I who were at the far end of the ward had climbed out of bed. The nurse however didn't appear to be duly concerned,, "Calm down Mr Fraser. No, I don't think you've had a heart attack. Now sit down and relax." "It's probably a bit of indigestion." It didn't sound like indigestion to us despite the fact that the hospital food was more than capable of delivering the symptoms within minutes of consumption. To Mr Fraser's credit he didn't give up. You could hear a mixture of anger and dismay in his weakened voice as he pleaded his case emphatically repeating the belief that he had endured an attack. Eventually the nurses, having now congregated and collaborated, made a decision and requested some back up. However it was a further 10 minutes before a registrar appeared, measured his blood pressure, oxygen, checked his ECG and his breathing and then proclaimed that he may well have suffered some form of mild seizure. He was whisked away to another ward within minutes. By this stage the nurse's attention had been drawn to sorting George out whose breathing now resembled the sound of dried autumn leaves being brushed on a frosty drive. With his nebuliser attached, he lay prostrate on the bed exhausted. We were all told to get back in to bed in a manner which implied we had misbehaved as if we were naughty school children. I wanted, like George and Peter, to mutter about the fact that it seemed to take a long time to deal with Mr Fraser. I bottled it however and before long peace had resettled in the ward.

Once lunch had been served later in the day it became apparent that both George and Peter had received food they had not ordered again. George was off within minutes muttering and complaining about the service, but to no one in particular. I was really beginning to admire him. As he derided the inefficiencies of the hospital catering department, he did so louder and louder and before he knew it, Pete joined in. Eventually a nurse arrived. It was becoming clear to me that both George and Peter were actually professional residents of the NHS. They appeared to be on the nurse's wanted posters as potential trouble makers. This was their third ward and they had crossed each other's paths on one other ward already. In total between them they had been in this hospital for a few weeks. "What's up with you two now?" she anxiously enquired. "It's no good" said George. "He's right," said Peter. It was becoming a double act. "Why can't some 'ets simple like what I want to eat get done proper. I'm fed up to the back teeth. It's always the same. What's up with them?" Peter chipped in, "I didn't eat mine. It were rubbish. I hadn't ordered sausage pie. It said Steak pie. That's what I ordered. Not sausage pie. There weren't any steaks in my pie. Just sausages!" "Are you sure?" asked the nurse. It was a fatal error on her part. Like two terriers with a rat they engaged and locked on. "Hey, this isn't the first time love. I'm always getting the wrong food. I know what a sausage looks like. I order one thing, get another. It isn't even eatable sometimes." "I'm a diabetic, you know," added George with such sanctimonious style that you could hear the defensive bristles on the back of the nurse's neck stand erect. "I should be getting good food that suits me. You know, diabetic stuff. You know." He reemphasised his point to a blank faced nurse who seemed to be extremely disinterested in pies. "I've asked to see someone loads of times but no one ever comes. Some stuff I can't eat. I've got diabetes, you know!" The nurse shrugged and with a hint of a shaking head reluctantly succumbed to the case for the prosecution. "Yes George, we know you're a diabetic. Ok I'll have a word and get something sorted, alright?" Peter grunted, "That'll be the day." I laughed rather too loudly, the nurse turned saw me listening, realised she was now surrounded and exited right at an alarming pace with a face suggesting shift end couldn't arrive soon enough.

They were quite right. The food was dreadful. I couldn't understand why the management of the trust didn't see the value of good nutrition and its contribution to our recuperation. At home within our own business we were involved in an NHS initiated trial delivering fruit to the workplace as part of the 5 a day programme. The NHS was funding the delivery of various fruit and vegetables in to selected companies with large staff numbers to see whether it was feasible to engage people at work to consume more fruit and vegetables if they were made readily available to them. Our job had been to source, prepare and deliver the fruit in to the workplace and present it for the work forces consumption. Everything from carrot sticks to grapes were included all set out in a communal work area ready for eating. A grab and snack policy if you like. Ironically I was in a hospital of the same trust, at the other end of the organisation. It was showing absolutely no interest in the dietary standards supplied to its patients, whilst back at work I was associating with the other end of the organisation that had the 5 a day programme at the very forefront of their minds. I never saw a piece of fruit given to a patient my whole time in the hospital. Ironically when I was discharged I was taken down to a waiting area and made ready for collection. There on a table stood a bowl of fresh fruit including some perfect bananas. I asked whether I was allowed one, which I was. As I consumed it I wondered why they were only available at the point of discharge when fresh fruit and vegetables would have been of so much more benefit to me and my compatriot patients as part of a healthy and wholesome diet during our recovery.

Throughout my incarceration I was constantly dismayed at the lack of joined up thinking between health and nutrition. It demonstrated a lack of imagination. In my head the 'You are what you eat' sound bite echoed between my ears. I thought about how many overweight and unhealthy people laid in the wards. I considered how financially important recovery time must be to the NHS in terms of achieving throughput by releasing beds sooner. I wondered how much the NHS trust was just cost focused in its budgetary formulation. I guessed that little management time was applied towards goal and objective setting and that there was literally no correlation between cost and efficiency. I bet my last dollar on the fact that no one ever referred to specialist dietary advisors in formulating menu selections and meeting exacting dietary requirements to aid the healing process. Yet here we all lay in a hospital trying to get better. Here were hundreds of human beings all totally reliant upon the food they ate to survive, never mind revitalize.

It seemed mindboggling and astonishing that no one with the authority for this department of the health service had instituted at least minimum requirements and standards as a target to improve performance. It was with an avid interest that I lay on my bed waiting to see what happened when staff came to meet George and Peter to address their grievances. George's diabetic condition and Peter's heart condition were significant health issues both of which were heavily dependent upon a constructive dietary input towards recovery. I had, despite the fact that my condition was clearly digestive in context, received absolutely no instruction or advice towards how I addressed food even in the short term. The two silly little girls who had attended to Barry and his dietary requirements had far from filled me with confidence. They seemed more interested in their own well being than Barry's. Whilst the jury was out I was leaning very much towards the prosecution's case of finding this hospital trust woefully guilty of a lack of due care and attention. Therefore I was not surprised by the fact that it was a member of the kitchen staff resembling 'Molly the Mop' still wearing her blue overalls and dirty kit who came up to the ward to talk to the increasingly militant faction of our ward.

As I understood it, the spread of infection was a very high risk issue within the health service and particularly in this hospital. The signs in the ward quite clearly stated that 'All visitors should refrain from sitting on the beds and should use the chairs provided.' It therefore seemed incredible to watch a member of the kitchen staff still wearing her grubby cooking work wear, circa 1985 with according stains, plonk herself down on George's bed as though she was at home in her own bedroom. There she remained and spent the next half an hour sitting on the edge of George's bed talking to the patient as if it was a casual chat over a pint down the local. Unfortunately, it turned out to be an uninspiring dialogue which was in no way about to influence policy within the organisation or the government. Nonetheless George was as good as any dispatch box MP. 'Do you know I'm a diabetic? I can only eat certain stuff. There ain't anything on them selection things you send round letting me know what's ok and what isn't. It's bloody stupid. I could eat sommets that makes me bloody ill.' Pete jumped in, "I keep ordering food and I get sommets else. It's happened loads of times. I'm bloody fed up with it. Sausage pie I got yesterday. Sausage pie. Who the hell puts a sausage in a pie? I can't cook but I reckon i could do a better job blindfolded than you lot do." It was certainly forceful campaigning stuff. They had my vote. I half expected the rather drab and under qualified representative of the kitchen staff to light a fag up and tell them to sod off if they didn't like it. Instead she fumbled about in her pockets and took out a rather dirty notepad and pen. 'Right let's get this down. Which meal did you order?" She spent 10 minutes arguing the toss with Peter about who might have put the wrong tray on the wrong trolley or delivered his meal to someone else as well as the value of sausage pie. The whole conversation highlighted how well qualified the catering staff were, and the fact that such a heinous crime as the delivery of the wrong tray must be someone else's fault. I was hardly surprised. It appeared that the kitchen staff were all angels but the delivery staff were all arseholes. Peter listened to the explanation and clearly felt better for getting it off his chest, the waif from the kitchen felt better because it was quickly established it couldn't be her or her departments fault. Everyone agreed it was someone else's fault and that they should probably be sacked. Item one was firmly resolved and it was now George's turn. 'That's all ok but I don't always want what's on the menu. There's nowt for me, you know, diabetics." "Oh but there is" trilled Sweeney Todd's accomplice and cook. "Look at the menu and you see we've put options. Low fat, low sugar, healthy option, so on. You just pick the right one. Simple!" She certainly was. I was struggling to hold a giggle in at the very mention of 'healthy option.' George rubbed his face with his enormously swollen hands. "You're missing the point love. What if I don't like that choice? I'm stuck. If the only option for me is sometts I can't stick, I'm bugared." "Ooh, right well that's easy. Just write down on the menu what you like and we'll cook it for you, ok?" "You what?" said Pete, "Do you mean if I want a cooked breakfast with bacon and eggs I can have it?" "We can't do fried eggs love. Scrambled is ok though." The two of them looked aghast. My jaw was slack as I took in what they had just been told. "We do it all of the time, you just need to know who to talk to." It was becoming clear that in the NHS 'it's not what you know it's who you know'. "Don't tell anyone else," she explained in a hushed voice, "cos they'll all want it, but I can do you a cooked if you want." I wondered just how long this clandestine operation would go unnoticed on a public ward. "Can I have it tomorrow," asked Pete. "Course you can love. I know the forms have gone round now but I'll sort you out." As she got up to leave having appeased her critics I wondered just how much good a fat soaked fry up was going to do for Pete's heart condition. It was clear that both George and Pete had been smitten by the vision in catering blue as they both sat and smiled like little children as they dreamt of their cooked breakfasts. Their health concerns were clearly not as urgent as their taste buds.

I was appalled. I felt like kicking up a stink of my own. As a farmer and food producer I was particularly unimpressed with the lack of care and attention shown towards the value of the meals produced within the hospital. I was disturbed by the lack of understanding or appreciation that food contributed to health. I was dismayed by the absence of quality, variety and healthy options. I was staggered by the lack of personnel focusing on dietary issues, particularly for patients with disorders dependent upon good dietary medical advice. Every week newspapers, TV news teams and politicians alike delivered stories about obesity, heart attacks, cancer and the failing social structures which we used to maintain our national diet. Each story would encompass the impact and cost to our health service and the taxpayers back pocket. Lyrical was waxed about how important it was to re-establish healthy eating and educate people towards healthy lifestyles. Yet here in the heart of the health service, the very place where the focus for such ideology should be fine tuned, there was no interest and no ambition evident to feed healthy food to recovering and ill patients. Somewhere within the management of the trust there would be an individual whose responsibility would be to determine the departmental direction of the catering facility for the entire hospital. They would need to balance budgets, manage staff, measure efficiencies, maintain equipment and standards and devise the menus and methods which ultimately resulted in what patients received on their plates three times a day. They would need to be qualified in catering management, have a vision of how to improve the department and be locked in to an objective which finely balanced the budget against delivering as wholesome and healthy a diet to patients and staff alike. I reflected that the shop window of the hospital, the A&E department, had been rather lacking in self belief themselves as they had all gone out for fish and chips rather than rely upon the hospital services. I looked at the curled up remains of my processed and inadequate turkey sandwich. Like a lot of other departments I had seen and experienced since entering the hospital it was clinically clear that the person in charge literally didn't give a shit.

The Golden Contract.

The weekend dragged on. No cleaners, few nurses, awful food and an environment as unfit for a healthy recovery as a battle field dressing station at Balaclava. The only relief came from my very welcomed visitors. Juliet, my wife, from whom I had separated back in July of last year, sat by my bed. It was wonderful to see her and to know that despite our incompatibility we cared deeply enough about each other that we both felt comfortable sat together talking about all of my recent experiences as if we were still happily married. She was supportive and concerned about my predicament. She always fell in to the 'Angel' category. She had brought me more news papers to read and various bits and bobs I was short of. She stayed for an hour or so and it gave us chance to catch up and to explain what I thought had happened to me. She held my hand and wished me well and asked to be kept informed of my progress, particularly with the results from my imminent colonoscopy. She was amazed to hear about my recent encounters with the hospitals inadequacies and whilst we whispered in hushed tones for fear of being overheard her occasional exclamation of 'God, really' tended to indicate I was telling her some shocking truths. The occasional prowling nurse hindered my stories and our abrupt silences gave the game away. Nonetheless it was good to be able to explain some of the concerns I had about the place and good to talk to her in particular. Once she had left, I as ever, felt a deep melancholy and a regretful space in my life. I busied myself with the weekend supplements she had brought with her to distract me from my potentially harmful and morose dive in to solitary despair.

The first thing I discovered was an article detailing the 'Golden Contract.' Just as I was about to really get stuck in to it, a nurse arrived to do the usual checkups. I wondered whether she was going to comment about my recent subversive conversations with Juliet. She eyed me suspiciously but didn't say anything. Everything seemed to be in order and as I thanked her and returned to my paper Doc 8 arrived. A junior Asian version of various doctors before him, he asked the same mandatory 20 questions. Before he could turn me into a 'Davi' I introduced myself and held out my hand which he shook. He checked my stats and asked how I felt. He wandered up the side of the bed and checked my pulse and asked whether he could examine my abdomen. Once he had finished he re-checked my stats and with a nod and a smile he wandered off up the ward to bother someone else. It was all a bit disappointing really. I had hoped for some ground breaking news as a result of his input; 'I think you will have twins' would have been something rather than the cursory nod. I had no idea what he wanted, what he was meant to be doing and what his role was. I had never seen him before and I never saw him again. I contemplated asking one of the nurses who he was but since none were evident I returned to my story. I wondered how much it cost to have someone like him wandering the wards at a weekend seemingly without a role.

I returned to the numerous stories about the NHS. GPs' rising salaries are part of a dramatic increase in spending on NHS pay. Last year, 47 per cent of all the extra spending on the NHS (£5.5bn) went on higher pay - for doctors, nurses and other staff. Hospital consultants earned £109,974 on average, up 27 per cent in three years. Nurses averaged

£27,868, a 12 per cent rise over the same period. I read on, intrigued and shocked by the staggering sums. It made me question what a GP was worth and how out of step with so many other important roles in society the medical profession had become. In an age when public sector pay increases, including the nurses were generally pinned back, yet board room raises of 30% were common there was some confusion within society what anyone was worth. As a farmer I was only too well aware of being undervalued. In Britain there is an ever increasing and dangerous diversity between wealth and poverty. City whizz kids bonuses of millions live in the same economy as minimum wage increases of 25 pence per hour. Nurses can't find affordable housing within the vicinity of the hospitals within which they work. Our lack of good nursing stock is hardly surprising when you consider that their cost of living prohibits their ability to hold a job down as a result of not being able to afford to live near the hospital within which they want to work. Yet GPs are earning an average of £106,000 a year as a result of Alan Milburn's ridiculous 'Golden contract.' GP earnings have risen by 63% in three years. At the same time they have given up out-of-hours work, home visits have become rare, and they work on average 44 hours a week which is comparatively low for top professionals in this day and age. Clinics and surgeries stay resolutely shut on evenings and at weekends, although GPs are pushing for a £20 surcharge to be applicable to patients accounts should they wish to arrange an out of hours appointment in the week . I knew I had picked the wrong career as medicine was fast becoming a license to print money. As I learnt more and more it seemed to me that it was no longer about a duty of care. In comparison, as a farmer, over the last 10 years I had worked for considerably less than a nursing wage working on average 75 - 100 hours per week, always being available at weekends and hardly finding time for holidays. In the last three years I had learned to live with unsustainable levels of profitability and bugar all disposable income. My whole focus had been about trying to build a larger more effective business, raising the bar in food production, quality assurance, resource management, cost of production as well as the management of our environment. It had all been at personal cost to me and yet at the same time for the benefit of the consumer. No one in the health service seemed willing to make the same commitment or sacrifice in their field. I couldn't understand how such a high priority profession in our society had escaped from the focus which was so important to it, we human beings who were dependent upon it.

The Healthcare Commission claimed that only a third of GPs took no appointment bookings more than two days ahead and 12% couldn't offer any appointments within two days. They earned more than the Lord Chancellor and circuit judges. But while their pay soared, they have been taking more NHS money into their own pockets and spending a lower proportion on their practices. They used to keep 40% for themselves, but in the past year that has crept up to 45%. As they're private businesses, no mechanism fixed how much they kept and what they invested in their clinics. Under Blair's relatively new philosophies on the health service patients were supposed to be the "market" that tested GP's quality. In my opinion patients neither feel nor behave like "customers" and most don't even know their GP is a business. We look at our health care services as a basic and fundamental structure in our society. We certainly do not expect to act as indicators in a profit driven market place. The Milburn contract has a guaranteed minimum income for GPs, so they can make as much profit as they like, with no risk of failure. There isn't even any comeback against less good GPs, the ones who are a bit lazy, weak, or bad managers or have simply lost interest.! Only the very worst are terminated as a danger to the public and that just seems a crazy situation.

The Milburn golden contract paid GPs for performing new tasks under a "quality framework". For example, they got extra points to identify chronic patients with kidney disease, diabetes or heart problems, so good early treatment might keep "frequent fliers" out of repeat hospital visits. The result last year was an extra 850,000 chronic cases being diagnosed, 100 more per practice, most with high blood pressure. This paid out some £70,000 extra to practices with maximum scores. According to the newspaper reports some suspected gross over-diagnosis, others said it showed the system worked. Either way, no one predicted such a sudden increase as the unexpected GP pay rises added £300m to NHS deficits. This illuminated all that was wrong with the way GPs were employed. Either they were cheating on payments or they had to admit they never bothered to check enough blood pressures until they were pretty much bribed to do so. Now GPs are demanding even more money to open their doors at times when the working public can actually visit. If you pay extra they might make an appointment to see you in the evening.

The ministerial response to this dilemma is for more private competition. For example, in Derbyshire, which had one weak GP area, the PCT offered a GP contract to a genuinely private company. There was uproar and a court challenge as GPs wanted to have it both ways, to be businesses when it suited but to be a loved and protected part of the NHS when that suited even better. A classic example of this is the deadlock over this year's pay awards. The GPs have appealed to the doctors' and nurses' pay review body. However the review body doesn't cover GPs because they are private contractors not NHS employees. Even so it suited GPs to pretend that they were part of the NHS.

It makes you wonder why GPs aren't paid a flat rate salary like consultants, with a normal job specification and the cash for their clinics safely ring-fenced. Blair probably won't do it however as he believed that they should have become genuinely competing private contractors in a real market. It will be interesting to see Brown's pitch on this one. In my opinion this idea would end up costing more than ever, with spare capacity in some areas and shortages in others and too little NHS control. Patients, unfortunately just don't make good enough choosers to guarantee a real market and they always want to trust their doctors even if eventually they don't. One way or another a different set up which doesn't cost the NHS so much money and inevitably doesn't detract from investment in patient care needs to be found quickly.

Once you begin contemplating the astronomical sums of money being drawn from the NHS budgets to fund individual's salaries and the cost of inept management of issues such as new IT emplacement within the NHS, the restrictive investment and poor conditions that exists in hospitals suddenly seems unsurprising, but extremely concerning. It seems incredible that no one is prepared to take the responsibility for improving patient care at the cost of hearing a few pompous and overpaid doctors and consultants whinging about their pay. I was aghast at the lack of forceful financial reality needed to pin back overspend on un needed administration and additional IT databases which in the scheme of things was well down on priority in comparison to Harold laying in his own shit night after night. I was utterly speechless at how out of control the NHS beast has become.

I found an article highlighting the issues of the 'Connecting to health' IT database more than alarming. The over spend to just rectify the problems of initiating the system in to the NHS may well lead to the costs being in excess of £20 billion. That isn't taking account of the initial outlay. A ludicrous, unimaginable and sickening amount of money, that in my opinion would be better directed towards funding an additional 40,000 nurses over a 10 year period rather than some valueless big brother concept which will keep hospital administrators more capable of hitting off the mark targets to achieve ill directed government funding. When you consider the redundancies being planned in hospitals in the north east of Yorkshire which will reduce facilities and beds it seems unbelievable that at the same time huge amounts of money are being spent on management, IT and admin. At least if the money was being directed to patient care, the people who have paid this staggering sum of money through taxation will receive something in return for it. They could lay in their beds, dying, suffering, reliant upon care, recovering, being cared for, and many being healed whilst experiencing care in a humane and dignified fashion with nurses and carers around them 24 hours a day, 7 days a week. I can't imagine any of us being that delighted that such a huge sum of money is in fact going to an IT company to deliver a service which we are unlikely to ever benefit from. As it stands the only improvement to life will be as a result of the time saved by the GPs and consultants so that they can go home earlier , play golf and then barbecue in their big houses and gardens and talk about their next holiday with their impressed mates.

By the time I had finished reading the various articles and considering all of the issues my blood needed measuring for temperature. It was a test I had yet to experience, but I knew if I was plugged in to a thermometer it would show 'boiling point' and spill out over the ward floor with all of the other muck and mess which lurked beneath the 1970's beds. What a catastrophe that would be as Mercury had just been banned in the use of thermometers and barometers in another of Blair's big brother moments. One of the worst parts about this huge waste of money in the NHS was the unbelievable lack of planning and management of the projects. It seemed that no one was accountable and if the right people with the right focus were in place much of it could be avoided. It all seemed such a terrible muddle.

I began scanning through the story in more detail. The company charged with rescuing the NHS's troubled IT system had consistently failed to meet its deadlines for introducing the project across the health service according to the papers.

Computer Sciences Corporation (CSC) was awarded a £2bn contract to take on a bigger role in overseeing the implementation of the Connecting for Health system, the biggest civilian computer project in history which is supposed to electronically link all doctors' surgeries and hospitals. But the government's hopes for CSC's £12.4bn project salvation had been hit by the news that the company had itself experienced huge problems. It was struggling to implement even the most basic parts of the project. According to its original business plan CSC was contracted to install new computer systems to 32 acute hospitals by April 2006. However, according to the NHS, only eight of the hospitals had received the basic 'administrative' systems by that date and the company had failed to deliver any working clinical systems which are the key part of the project which is supposed to record a person's medical data electronically. Nearly three years into the project, CSC continue to miss their targets, due in part to problems with the software provided by iSoft, the troubled IT company currently being investigated for accounting irregularities. A letter from Guy Hains, president of CSC Europe, to Gordon Hextall, chief operating officer for Connecting for Health, written earlier this year, promised six more hospitals would get new computer systems by the end of October this year. But of these only two had received a system; the remainder looked like they would miss the deadline.

In an interview a spokeswoman for CSC confirmed the delays. 'A small number of Trusts within the North West & West Midlands cluster have opted to revise their dates to await future software release,' she said. This revelation will raise fears that the project will not come in on time and, as a result, will go further over budget. Critics suggested that the eventual cost to the taxpayer of fixing the system's myriad problems will push the total bill for Connecting for Health to in excess of £15 bn. Some have suggested it will rise even further to as much as £20bn.

As I finally put down the news papers all I wanted to do was kick Patricia Hewitt up her thorny and ridiculously chatty arse. I was extremely angry; mad. I sat and shook my head in disbelief at what I had learnt. A nurse walked through the ward. She obviously spotted my ruddy complexion and rather angry expression. "You ok love?" I stared across the ward looking at a wall very hard. I breathed in deeply and sighed. As I shook my head I swore, "Do I look alright? Would I be here if I was alright? No I'm bloody not alright." It took a few minutes to explain that I was angry with just about everything. My missed opportunities, my lack of progress in the hospital, the state of the health service etc etc. She looked bewildered and for a moment fell silent deep in thought. Eventually after some delicate thought she suggested that I stopped reading the papers as they were always full of bad news and "watch a bit of telly instead." I could gauge that it wasn't the done thing to lie in an NHS bed and start taking up a nurse's time whinging about the crazy situation which existed in the very institution I lay in. I switched on the TV. It was the news. An NHS trust was being investigated for financial irregularities and a lady suffering from dementia had died in a mix up when she had been returned home without care. I switched it off. I was running out of things to do. The nurse had kindly fetched me some water in a jug and she had humorously suggested I used it to cool down. I hadn't even smiled. I took a sip and looked around the ward for somewhere to bury my head with all of the other ostriches.

The same nurse had started setting up a pump next to George's bed and had entered in to a rather left wing conversation on how much better things were now than in the olden days. I wasn't sure whether it was a direct reaction to my earlier comments or whether they were just two souls from the same background. She had recently been on holiday in Egypt with her husband and had enjoyed it so much she was planning on going back within the next few months. "It's a lot better now i'nt it luv, you know, we can do as we like more than before, like." "Yeah" replied George, "I can afford to do all sorts I didn't used to be able to." The nurse continued, "Yeah, unless you were rich like, or your parents had loads of money, you couldn't do owt like. There weren't any opportunities, just jobs and work. It's a lot easier now. You don't have to work so hard and you can get paid a lot more. I get loads more holidays in now. Last year we went to Egypt and we're off again in a couple of weeks. I like going to Egypt. " I reminded myself never to go and see the pyramids.

Colonoscopy.

A Monday morning had never come around fast enough in my opinion. In the outside world that we all called normality, the weekend was special. As a farmer I had never really experienced this phenomena as whether it was a weekday or weekend the weather determined our work rate and output. Over the last few years I could count the number of full weekends I had not been at work on one hand. In the last year and up to breaking ranks with my role in the family business I had not taken one weekend off. However to most people that Monday morning feeling was one everyone related to. The weekend was a fun, family time with leisure and rest or a time for catching up with the household chores or threatening the garden with a mower. The dreaded return to work at the beginning of another week always emphasized our dislike for Mondays. However in hospital it was despite the many visits from friends and family over the weekend the exact opposite. The weekend had been the Armageddon of our hospitalization and the return of Monday morning brought with it the return of good staff and normality. Rosie breezed in with a smile and with her sleeves rolled up, told us what she had been up to and enquired after each and every one of us, making the place feel under control again. The very atmosphere of concern created by the weekend's inefficiencies evaporated as the team of nurses and cleaners dispensed with the weekend's mess. Rosie was 'Angel' category.

I had been lined up over the weekend for my procedural examination. My colonoscopy diet had included, just for a change, nil by mouth since lunch time on Sunday and the rather bland and curled up turkey sandwich. I was now prepared for a dreaded internal assessment. I had forgotten one small thing however, which jumped into clear view as I was presented with a suspicious looking lemon drink at breakfast. Everyone else tucked in to their newly acquired cooked breakfast with additions of "do you want milk and sugar with that?'" I studied the warm drink in front of me. It had been delivered by a busy nurse without an explanation. "You'll need to drink that" was all I had heard. Rosie noticed that I wore a puzzled expression. As she came over I asked whether it was what I thought it might be. It unfortunately was and in Rosie's opinion many people paid considerable sums at health farms to receive the same treatment. I laughed. It was a cleansing experience in a glass slightly lacking the comfortable surroundings of a health farm. I reluctantly drank the contents of the glass not looking forward to its results. It was refilled for my enjoyment a second time.

Sal, another highly competent nurse, was busy with Barry. He hadn't looked well at all when he went past the end of my bed to go to the bathroom. The curtains remained drawn around his bed and Rosie had also poked her head round to see what was up. Before much longer a doctor appeared to talk to Barry as well. After several minutes of discussion and a phone call from the nurse's station to the resident dieticians a conclusion was reached. Some hours later Barry sat in the chair next to my bed recounting the dreadful weekend he had suffered.

On Friday afternoon the hospital staff had coordinated his care for the weekend. His consultant had discussed his overall condition with him including his intake of food and drugs. A registrar or doctor had subsequently discussed his nursing care with the nursing staff. His situation with acute Crohns and a colostomy bag required an intensive management of his dietary intake. However what they had all forgotten was a need to address his fluid intake as a result of the changes they had made to his diet. Over the weekend despite drinking fluids, Barry found himself fading. The weaker he became the less he drank and inevitably ate. He became fragile and tired. Feeling a bit isolated and unwell he had also become rather insular and withdrawn. By Monday morning he had struggled to get out of bed and when he had walked to the bathroom he had felt faint and light headed. Although he had avoided fainting and recovered reasonably quickly, he reported his declining health to one of the nurses. The reason for his decline was that he had not received any intravenous fluid since Friday afternoon and for two days and nights he had become seriously dehydrated. In an ever decreasing circle he had consumed less and less food and fluid as he became weaker over a period of time. Although the morning discussion and inquest around Barry's bed had finally highlighted that he hadn't received the necessary fluid it had taken a long time for anyone to notice his condition. He should have been on three or four units of saline drip each day and yet no one was clear why this hadn't been done. It appeared that a lack of communication between the doctor who had seen him on Friday, the nurses on the Friday afternoon shift and the nurses coming onto shift Friday night and subsequently the weekend had resulted in the message not getting through. Incredibly within an hour of receiving his first fluids he had responded and within a few hours felt back to normal. As I sat and listened to Barry I wondered what normal meant. Whilst I felt unwell, my condition shrank into insignificance in comparison. He shook his head in disbelief as he told the story. At one point late in to Sunday night he had decided he might be really ill and on the way to dying. He couldn't organize himself properly and had become extremely disorientated. Whilst he had mentioned feeling ill over the weekend to staff on the ward on a couple of occasions no one had put two and two together. He felt weaker and weaker and thus less able to manage his condition or find the energy to eat or drink. It had in fact been Barry's suggestion, as he lay in his weakened state during the Monday morning inquest, to consider the lack of fluids as being the cause for his feeling unwell. It was not from a considered medical opinion, but just from the experience of feeling unwell before when his fluid intakes had varied with his diet. As he got up to go and head back to his window view, he said something profound. It has stuck with me ever since. "If the boot was on the other foot I would hope I would show more interest in them than they do me. I'd like to see them handling this. It might teach them a thing or two." It would indeed be an interesting experience for all of the medical staff in a hospital to be treated as a patient for a day or two in a hospital within which they were not known. If they were admitted for a superficial procedure or examination but remained dependent upon the entire medical infrastructure for their well being for 48 hours I wonder what they would learn from their experience and bipolar view of the NHS in action.

I had noticed throughout our chat on the opposite side of the ward that George was not particularly happy either. He had been picking away at his stomach for some time. A hand sized red rash had appeared on his belly. Sal was passing and she was called in to investigate. "I don't know what it is but it's been pestering me the last couple of days" broadcasted George. "Mmm, that's odd" declared Sal, "have you had anything medical done to you recently in this neck of the woods?" "No" replied George, "the last thing I had done were a biopsy about three year ago." His raspy broad accent was in stark contrast to Sal's educated voice and accentuated the fundamental disbelief in her reply. "Did they stitch you up afterwards George?" "I reckon they did, aye, they did!" "Did you have the stitches taken out?" Silence reigned for a few seconds as George contemplated the error. "Well George it appears that you never had the stitches taken out." "Bloody hell" uttered George, "you mean I've ad them buggers in all that time?" "It would seem so. I'll nip and fetch the scissors." Sal quickly returned and within the blink of an eye had cut out the three stitches. "By eck, that feels a lot better" proclaimed George to all of the ward. "Good job you are on the NHS and I don't charge for minor operations, eh George?" Sal cheekily, smiled. There wasn't much else you could say really. It made me wonder how much George suffered from his condition to have put something like old itchy stitches into such a minority. I wondered whether his nervous system worked effectively and whether he could feel anything at all. It was a bizarre few minutes but it again emphasised how very ill some of these people were and how in particular diabetes can run and ruin your life. To see people who are long term sick and totally dependent upon care for their sustainable well being reinforced my opinion that they were pretty marvellous to be able to deal with some of the conditions the NHS threw at them.

As my day wore on I proceeded to develop a Linford Christie start from my blocks so that I could maintain my dignity as the lemon drink did its job. I was beginning to concern myself as to whether I would be seen, as like the day I had received my endoscopy, time marched on and the afternoon had all but disappeared. I couldn't face another day of having nothing to eat or going through the clear out process again. Doc 9 turned up at about the point I had decided I was about to become another bed blocking statistic. "Mr Davi?", he asked pronouncing my name with a harsh rather than a soft 'a'. I explained it was 'Davey' with an 'e' and pronounced as so and had been since at least 1756 which was when I could trace back my descendants from just down the road. He missed the point and settled in to his questions. Not quite 20 but near enough to become bored after the first 3. I was beginning to think about giving false answers to see whether it created a different management of my condition. Once he had established I was who I was and that I was going for a colonoscopy, (and he only had to ask), he questioned me about my recent 100metre sprinting and whether I had finished and was ready to go down for my procedure. I was ready and once we had agreed on everything he informed me that a porter would be with me shortly. I waited for about half an hour and sure enough the same guy with his radio in his hand as had transported me before turned up. "Yeah, receiving. Arrived at ward, Collecting and then setting off with patient. Over." I expected either a small team of the SAS to break cover and recce the corridors ahead for the Taliban or for him to light his after burner as we exited the flight deck with several Gs pulling at my neck muscles. Oddly enough the terrorists remained hidden and both 'Goose' and 'Ice' our wing men remained below deck. We set off at walking pace and after collecting my notes 'Maverick, me and the bath chair with my dignity protected by the notes and by keeping my knees close together headed for my procedure. I really loved those hospital gowns.

As we travelled down the corridors and lift shafts into another part of the bowels of the hospital I started to flick through the now quite thick file that sat on my knees. It wasn't long before 'Maverick' noticed what I was doing. "You shouldn't be looking at those. You're not allowed." I was intrigued. "Really, but they are my notes!" "I know like, but I'm not supposed to let you look at em, like." "Why?" "Well if there's any stuff in there like, that you don't agree with or that you might thinks wrong, like , you could sue someone like." I kept looking. "You can get a copy if you go through channels, but you're not allowed to look now, like." I wondered if they would read the same as they did now by the time I got a copy. Apart from the daily charts which covered the various aspects of all of the measurements of my observations there were dozens of sheets of paper with typically bad hand writing on. Again I thought that there seemed little point in giving them pens as they hardly used them and when they did they were found to be illiterate. It really is amazing how much we pay people who can't write. On the reports which went back to my admission in to A & E hasty notes had been scribbled in to boxes. Everything from my initial symptoms, the ludicrous diagnosis of dysentery, my loss of consciousness, my moves from one ward to the next, my treatments, a good deal about my transfusion, to various theories about ulceration of the stomach. There were various charts including a stool chart. I wished I had a pen as I was keen to draw a piece of furniture on my graph to see whether anyone actually paid any attention to the information already scribbled on the form. I could see several different contributions from several different doctors and consultants alike. Paragraphs of different handwriting on different sheets of paper stuffed in to the file. It looked disjointed and it highlighted to me the confusion and lack of communication you feel you are receiving as a patient as you travel through the system. "Now come on like, you shouldn't be looking. We're nearly there." I folded the covers together and considered just how much information and opinion existed about my experience. I was still no further on to finding out what was the matter with me or what had caused it all. "Here we are mate. Arriving with patient to be scoped. Dropping off. Back to main doors in 10. Over." With his GPS set and all pre flight checks achieved, Maverick pointed his chair east and disappeared from view. I was sure he tipped his wings in a departing gesture as he rounded the corner and fell out of sight. I was in the same department as when I received my endoscopy. I found the waiting room and waited.

The best part of the day had gone and 5 o'clock had disappeared before a young nurse arrived to check me over and ask me several pre op questions. Once I had passed the test she decided it would be a good idea to put another canula in. I had only just managed to have the old ones taken out. I explained this to her but it was an irrelevancy as far as she was concerned. It seemed I would need one for them to be able to administer drugs during the procedure. I bet her that she couldn't get it in the same hole. She didn't laugh but I found it quite funny . Once she had found one of my veins which were starting to feel like well used motorways, she inserted the canula and I was moved through to meet Con 2. He shook my hand and asked how I was feeling. "Tired" was as much as I could achieve. It didn't seem to impress him much but I didn't feel like expanding. He professionally guided me through his intended course of action which was exactly how I would have expected to be treated. He mentioned that he would be going through the large intestine and then into the ileum as that was the area he thought was worth investigating for Crohns disease. My immediate thoughts turned to Barry and I started to shiver. He explained that dependent on what he might find the next course of action may well be a trip to Harley Street and a camera capsule to help diagnose the exact issue I was suffering from. Barry leapt in to my mind again. He explained that he was going to use air to blow up the bowel and relaxant to restrict the bowels natural palpitations so that examination was made easier. It sounded like the same thing that happened when you went out and drank a lot of beer. I was administered a relaxant nonetheless through my IV and then asked to read and sign a disclaimer. "Yes you can rupture my bowel without risk of being sued now," I thought as I signed the document.

I decided that since this was the point to which I had been focused on for the last 8 days it would be best to take advantage of the moment and learn as much as I could about my condition and the eventual prognosis. I started asking various questions. What are we looking for, what are we likely to find, what will be the outcome should xyz become apparent. Con 2 became very reserved. Rather than answer he dismissed my interested questioning and advised that it would be more appropriate to wait and find out what the problem was, rather than worry about it at this stage. I shut up!

I was put up on to an operating trolley and asked to lie on to my side. Within a few seconds I had a colonoscopy tube invading my back passage with an unenviable amount of discomfort. The relaxant wasn't making me feel very relaxed. Above my head a television screen, to which Con 2 had become absorbed, as was I, displayed the journey of the scope through my bowel. It was quite extraordinary to watch the inside of your body on a television screen. Everything appeared normal. As the scope carried on its journey Con2 muttered about more air and more drugs as palpitations in the bowel were not lending themselves to a clear examination. Once he was happy with his visual on the screen the scope carried on further. The inflated pink inner lining of my large intestine seemed untroubled by any flaws and as it appeared healthy Con 2 accelerated the passage of the scope through my body. He finally reached the point where the large intestine joined the small intestine. Con 2 explained that he was about to go into the small intestine and that it may become slightly more uncomfortable. For a short while the scope busied itself trying to find the entry point. A bit like a car at a busy roundabout, it spent a while pushing and nudging to find a gap. Eventually folds of tissue exposed an entry in to the small intestine and the scope entered the ileum. Within seconds it was clear that more inflammation existed in this part of the bowel. After travelling up the ileum for a few centimeters small ulcerations were evident on the lining of the gut. The scope turned a corner and suddenly staring back at us was a large red ugly ulcer which had clearly perforated and bled. "Ah Hah" pronounced Con2. "This looks like the culprit. Ok Biopsy. " The scope turned from camera function to sample collecting function as a small rod with calipers extended from its nose like something out of a space walk. It snipped a small piece of flesh from the ulcered area and protracted back to its base. This was repeated three times. "Need to check the tissue samples for any nasties", Con 2 informed me. The thought of what nasties might include concerned me. After exploring a little higher up and finding nothing further he began to move the scope out of the bowel. Whilst it had seemed only seconds it had in fact taken over twenty minutes to complete the procedure. I was very relieved it was over.

As Con 2 pulled the scope from my body with a concerning speed he began his prognosis, formed from his observations. "Nasty ulceration, bound to be the point of the bleed. Don't think you need to wonder where the bleed came from! It could be various things. I observed some narrowing of the ileum; its typical of crohn's symptoms. Anyway, let's get you back up to the ward. It's getting late. I'll be up to see you tomorrow. I think you could go home." I could have kissed him.

I had hoped I would be able to get back up to the ward as soon as possible as I was very tired, so I listened intently for the sound of 'Maverick's' two way radio scattering messages about his location. A nurse helped me off the bed, transferred me to a bath chair and wheeled me into a recovery room. "You'll have to stay here a bit and let nature take its course love." It suddenly dawned on me that the increasing pressure in my abdomen was heading south. A very large and spotty nurse offered me biscuits and conversation. I wasn't sure whether I should be eating them but refused to concern myself as I was extraordinarily hungry. I realized that I would have to wait for Maverick and his amazing flight deck manoeuvres. I listened to her problems both at work and at home. I wished I could turn her off as a bit of peace and quiet whilst the air inserted by Con 2 dispersed would have been welcome.

The first raspy tornado exited the bed sheets with such force that the nurse stopped talking about her 22 stone ex boyfriend who had gone to work in South Africa. She looked startled for a moment, then giggled and offered me another biscuit. It appeared very little was going to force her off the subject or out of the room. Over the next hour I listened to the torrid tale of her life in nursing college, her series of ex lovers which I am convinced were firmly in her imagination, the problems she had with her ex boyfriend who was actually sleeping with another nurse whom she had two timed with a previous boyfriend which caused a terrible stink and had led to them being posted to different hospitals a result. I was wishing I could cause a terrible stink as well as it might be the only way of getting rid of her. Once it became clear that I wasn't that interested in her 'between the sheets' activities she started fiddling with her mobile phone and scanning her texts. I was about to bring myself to asking her why as patients we were not allowed our phones and yet the staff were, when she started reading me some of the jokes she had recently received. After several 'Top Gear' gags and a few about Saddam Hussein losing his head, and lots of giggling on her part, she asked whether I had any jokes. I was rather reluctant to encourage her but nonetheless had a perfect one which I knew would leave her in stitches. At a medical convention a male doctor and a female doctor started eyeing each other up straight out of a script from Holby City. He asks her to dinner which she accepted. After dinner one thing lead to another and they ended up in bed together. Just as they are about to get into some serious love action the female doctor gets up and goes to wash her hands. She comes back and makes passionate love with her male doctor but immediately afterwards gets up again and goes and washes her hands. As she comes back to bed for the second time the doctor says to her "I bet you're a surgeon". "Yeah that's right I am, how did you guess?" "Well you are always washing your hands." She then says, "Well I bet you're an anesthesiologist." "Amazing" said the male doctor, "How did you guess?" "Easy" she said, "I didn't feel a thing."

I knew it was a mistake by the fact that she very nearly tripped up over the next door trolley. She laughed so hard that when she leant backwards she lost her balance and for a moment reenacted a Torville and Dean routine over the shiny floor surface. To boot I let out another enormous fart which set her off again. Once she recovered some two minutes later she started asking for jokes. Could I text her and whether she could have my phone number; I let go of my biggest fart yet. It was well timed as it was sufficiently violent for even her liking and she made an excuse about getting some transport organized and disappeared behind the curtain. It appeared that I had got away with it.

As time and everything else passed I realized just how very tired I was. I began to feel drowsy despite a continuing abdominal pain and a fair bit of occasional noise from below the sheets. The next thing I knew was that the very large spotty face was shaking me by the shoulder and asking me to climb in to a bath chair as it was time to go up to the ward. It was in fact 8.40 pm. I climbed in to the chair and we set off. She was straight back in to the story about the boyfriend nursing in South Africa and that she thought that since this hospital was so crap and that she missed him so much she might join him sooner than later. I asked her to elaborate on crap. As she pushed me in the bath chair via the back route through the service corridors and store rooms and up service elevators, I couldn't help but notice the decay and dirt which littered the walls, floors and ceilings. "Well, the pay's crap and the hours are crap. The facilities are crap and none of my friends are here. I'm just not very happy really and I want to get into proper nursing, you know on a ward. No one seems to care much round here." Despite my reservations about her it seemed that she had a genuine passion for nursing. Whether she would ever be any good at it was another question. As we arrived back on to the ward after journeying what seemed for hours through the bowels of the hospital but had only been fifteen minutes, I could feel my head nodding again. I had barely transferred myself from the bath chair to the bed and said goodbye to the large spotty one, when as my head hit the pillow I fell to sleep. I was pleased to be on my own again.

Goodbyes.

I woke up knowing that for the first time since my admission I would be able to eat a normal meal. I knew I wouldn't be worrying about having to lose everything I had eaten in preparation for a procedure. A bowl of breakfast cereal tasted like food from heaven itself. However it wasn't all good news, as I had slept as badly as ever. Harold had unfortunately interrupted my sleep with his discomfort and noise again. He had moaned and cried out in the night. A nurse on the late shift had investigated and then with help spent a while cleaning him up. With that and George's sleep talking, Barry's insomnia and Pete's snoring, sleep had been hard to maintain. I wasn't going to miss the sleeping arrangements much. George had been rambling for minutes on end about a car chase in which he eventually was stopped by the police. He delivered a one sided conversation as if he was actually being interviewed by a policeman declaring his innocence and stating that he had never gone over 40 miles an hour. "Come on mate, you know it wasn't me; couldn't be me speeding., cos I've got no license and no insurance. " I had chuckled despite my aching and tired body.

I hadn't been awake long when Mum called. Sadly she was the bearer of bad news. Before she called, despite being tired, I was quite upbeat at the prospect of escaping what had become a bizarre and detached experience and I was so looking forward to getting home. The news was about Bramble. As I had been suffering at the hands of Con 2 and his colonoscopy, Bramble had been fighting her last battle with her infection which had been gradually deteriorating ever since I had admitted myself in to hospital. Dad had finally made the decision that she was suffering too much and taken her in to the vets who had put her to sleep. The news quickly took the gloss off my day, as she was one of several puppies, my old lab Pepper had delivered in early November of 1991. I had watched her birth and missed her death. There wasn't much left of my old life and she had been a fond memory of the last 15 years. She had been born the year Juliet and I became engaged and her passing felt like further closure on an episode in my life which had recently become harnessed with layers of sadness. 15 was a very good age for a Labrador but as everyone knows their passing is never easy despite the pleasure you have with them and I found this moment particularly difficult under the circumstances. I decided to head off for a shower so that I could at least mourn her passing with a degree of privacy.

Once I was back in my bed, refreshed and composed, Sal turned up to administer what had become my daily prescription by IV to treat my inflamed 'Chron's' affected bowel. She checked my vital signs. With baited breath I waited to hear that everything was in order and that she could see no reason why I couldn't go home. I asked her to find out when that might be so that I could arrange for someone to collect me. She didn't come back. In the mean time, Peter was collected by 'Maverick' with his radio churning out more instructions than Montgomery on D Day. He was away to have a cardio catheter examination to learn more about his heart condition. I waved to him and gave him a thumbs up as he was wheeled away with the two way blaring confirmation that 'ETA to cardio in 15; out'. You had to smile. I picked up the newspaper and tried to find something to take my mind off not hearing about when I could go home. As ever there was plenty on the NHS. Another story detailing the £12 billion upgrade of the NHS IT system seemed more than relevant. I wondered what you could achieve in the NHS with £12 billion if you spent it on something other than IT. The health minister, Lord Hunt, defending the government's position declared that once completed, 117,000 doctors, 397,500 nurses and 128,000 scientists and therapists could be connected to bring benefits to 50 million patients. It made you wonder what they were all doing right now and whether their patient's well being was at the forefront of their minds. I somehow doubted it. After an hour passed I asked about my departure again. There seemed to be a degree of confusion about whether I could be discharged and when it might happen. A hospital pharmacist arrived and dispensed some blister packs of the same drug I had been receiving intravenously to continue treating my small intestine once I got home. I asked her to find out when I might be allowed to go home. I couldn't really understand what the problem was. My mind started drifting towards various potential problems which might be causing the delay such as a new diagnosis, subsequent treatments or even further investigations. Perhaps there would be some worrying news that might have evolved from my colonoscopy biopsy. I was starting to enjoy the day less by the hour. I continued to hear nothing from anyone to either confirm or allay my concerns, including a drop in from Con 2 which he had promised me. I was still in the dark as to what had caused my illness. It was clear that some form of ulceration of the ileum had ruptured and bled very badly. What I needed to know was why it had formed and why it had become so acute. By 11.45 am I was still in the dark and I was just beginning to think I would never escape when Doc 10 appeared by my bedside like a genie out of a bottle.

After an initial introduction he asked me the 20 questions. I wasn't going to miss them. I thought I would be able to recite them for life or even use them as an interview technique in the future. I began to assume he was just another passing medic who was doing the rounds through the wards and I wondered who on earth allowed such valuable resources to be so badly deployed. However something changed in his demeanor. He began asking me very pertinent questions about the life history of my health. He listened to the answers and asked further probing questions. I suddenly realized that for the first time since I had entered the hospital I had someone showing exactly the right approach to investigating my condition. Here was a doctor who showed respect for his patient, held a normal one to one conversation and had a genial bedside manner unlike some of his Attila the Hun confederates. He wanted to know about various opinions and diagnoses from other consultants and doctors I had been under over the years. He asked me about my procedures whilst in hospital during the last week and finite detail about my symptoms prior and post to my admission. He shook his head in disbelief when I mentioned the dysentery and assured me that this wasn't an infectious problem. We eventually rounded onto Con 2's very recent colonoscopy and the analysis of his observations. He explained that the strictures and ulceration were in line with symptoms typical of crohn's disease but the biopsy results could be more conclusive with clearer diagnosis possible once they were evident. He carried on and I wondered where he might be taking the conversation. He kept asking questions about my health and recent history. He considered my recent personal life and the changes I had experienced, but made no comment, rather unlike Con1 at the beginning of my admission. Eventually he directed his enquiry towards my very recent past and the operation I had undergone in December. My hydrocele and epididymtis condition had resulted in a prescription of anti inflammatory drugs which as soon as I mentioned them he looked me in the eye like a hawk spotting a mouse. "When, how many, and any other drugs?" he immediately asked. I continued by telling him about my broken ribs and my dependency for a while at least prior to my anti inflammatory prescription on other ibuprofen pain relief. He was fascinated by this period. I couldn't understand why. I asked him to explain the connection and as he detailed the impact that these drugs can have on your bowel my bottom jaw hung in disbelief. Ibuprofen in various forms can cause serious and in some cases fatal bleeding from the stomach or intestines. It was the first time anyone had even mentioned this as a possible reason for my illness despite me mentioning my stay in hospital in December and my broken ribs to every doctor I had seen whilst I had been in. His opinion developed and he suggested that considering I had such a history of IBS and probably an underlying mild case of IBD I would be even more prevalent to possible side effects from aggressive drugs such as Ibuprofen. I began to think back to how I had felt since my rugby injury and my visit to hospital in December. It was difficult to pick out any particular moment but I recognized that there had been a period when I had started feeling more tired and more unsettled in the tummy department sometime prior to my operation before Christmas. As I latched on to his explanation and asked more detailed questions Doc 10 was quick to broaden the debate. It was an option, a possibility. It may be that they were not involved or only played a minor role and that a particular type of Crohn's (there wouldn't just be one would there) was the culprit. Whatever the actual cause he felt confident that it was within this domain and probably caused by a combination of reasons. He felt that I was on the mend as my obvious recent symptoms had improved and my haemoglobin levels whilst still not quite right were sufficiently repaired to indicate a more healthy perspective. He explained that Con 2 would be in touch at some point in the near future and that it was ok to arrange my departure and escape home. I genuinely thanked him for his interest and time and for the first time in several days felt as though the NHS had shown its potential. As he left I asked him to find out when I could be picked up. He promised to chase it up.

By 12.30 pm I was beginning to think I had been forgotten again when Sal popped her head around the ward door and suggested I get dressed as someone would be up to take me to the discharge room shortly. I made a hurried call home to make sure someone could collect me and started getting changed. As I packed a few frugal belongings into my bag I realized that my bedside flowers brought in by one of my visitors were not going home with me. I picked them up and walked over to give them to Barry. As I placed them on his table and wished him all the best he handed me a couple of motoring magazines he'd finished reading for me to take home in a trade like gesture. He was on good form considering everything and he was hopeful of some more news on a speedier outcome to his corrective surgery. He kindly asked after my prognosis and I told him about my possible crohn's. As I shook his hand and wished him luck he plucked out of his bedside draw a small canister containing a camera capsule. "They let me keep it. Take it out. Have a look." I took out the amazing piece of technology, no larger than a multi vitamin capsule, and looked at it with some suspicion. I wondered how much of Barry's life had been affected by this contraption and its interrupted journey through his body. "That thing has a lot to answer for. Make sure you don't end up the same way" he said, concerned about me. After a final farewell and wishing each other luck I walked back down the ward saying goodbye to George and Peter as well as Harold who was as ever asleep. George was wearing his nebulizer and raised his hand. His cherry legs lay on top of the bed and as ever he looked uncomfortable, even so, he offered me a smile from under the mask. Peter was recently back from his investigatory procedure. As I shook his hand I asked how he had got on earlier in the day. "Uh, it's bloody typical I'm going to have to go to another hospital now because they can't do the next procedures here. I went down to have an angio but they couldn't do it. I've been in here nearly an extra week; since last Thursday. I was only in over the weekend so I could be seen on Monday morning. Then they cancelled and pushed it through to today. They are transferring me tomorrow. How long after that, only knows. What a waste of time." I shook my head and agreed with him. I wished him luck and returned to my corner of the ward. I had only sat on my bed for a minute before a nurse arrived. There were none of the staff who had looked after me on the nurse's station to thank and say good bye to, so I followed her down through the hospital for endless miles until we found ourselves outside a converted ward with beds stacked up in the corner and two settees and a television placed in the middle of the room. She left me there sat staring at daytime TV waiting for someone to collect me. I couldn't believe I was going home or that I had probably become number 120,000th person in the UK diagnosed with Crohns. I sat in the waiting room and plugged away through the papers again. A brilliant headline caught my eye, National Hypocrisy Service. Allegedly 28% of GPs have private medical insurance and 33% prefer private treatment. Civil servants at the department of health are entitled to become members of the Benenden Healthcare Society which serves one million BT, Post office and civil service workers and their families. If they fall ill they are treated at a private hospital in Kent with tennis courts and a swimming pool. More than half of the TUC's members hold some form of private medical insurance, a higher proportion than any other socio-economic group in the UK. Various stories abound about MP's and cabinet ministers families being treated with privileged care with consultants waiting at the door to meet them as they arrive at the hospital. Rather different to my experience and the experiences of the millions of normal patients within the NHS. As with so many of the stories I had read whilst I lay amidst the NHS this one struck a chord. A point made in the story and one which had occurred to me time and time again was that how do the people responsible for the management of the NHS make decisions when they have so little experience of being sick, helpless and ignored on a dirty NHS ward?

It was with a great feeling of relief that I spied Mum as she walked across the entrance of the ward. I raised my hand so that she spotted where I was sitting. I stood up and kissed her. She was desperate to obtain a proper release form as evidently there was some benefit obtainable from the state as a result of my incapacity which the form enabled efficient application. I felt de-mob happy and about as interested in a form as Ben Cohen was in tackling Jonah Lomu in 1996. I just wanted to get home. Mum had other ideas. Her first port of call, the nurse's station just outside the discharge waiting area, led to a number of blank faces. It was clear that such a form had to be obtained from a specific department which Mum set off to at a gallop with assurances that she would return. Before I could lend any opinion I was back on my own with Fern Britton and Philip Schofield for company.

After a quarter of an hour had frittered away and I had learnt something about spring fashions for size 14's Mum returned clutching a small slip of paper. I picked up my bag and walked out of the ward and along the corridors of the rabbit warren. As I walked past the wards and treatment rooms I looked into them. Rows of very similar people with many ailments sat in wards just like the one I had left. People sat in chairs waiting to be seen. Long faces and misery generally peered back. I felt like I was letting them down because I was escaping. As I walked out of the hospital main entrance and into a cool clear January day and felt the weak winter sun on my face I thanked god that I was alive and that I had been given a second chance. I felt as though I had been incarcerated in the bowels of a third world prison in an almost 'Bridget Jones' drugs mix up. It was a magnificent feeling to walk towards the car and sit in it. The sun was warmer through the glass; I closed my eyes, breathed deeply and let out the loudest sigh in the history of man. I was going home.

The select committee.

As I arrived home and the car stopped in the drive, I looked about my garden and couldn't believe how much I had missed it in such a short time. I felt as though I had been away a year never mind just over a week. I let myself in to the house and immediately went to the office. A great pile of mail rested on my desk; I opened up the computer and downloaded dozens of e mails. There was great comfort in reattaching myself to my old life.

The fridge looked rather bleak but fortunately mum had gone to the trouble of stocking up with a few essentials. After half an hour and making sure I was ok she said her goodbyes and headed home to leave me to my very quiet and dog-less existence. Dad had buried Bramble in the garden and I went outside to say goodbye. A neat mound of fresh earth just a few yards from where her mother lay clearly showed where she rested. I put my hand on the top of the soil and said a little prayer. Between us we had been through the mill recently and I was just so pleased the roles had not been reversed. I thought about all of the good times we had experienced together. The best had been an amazing retrieve of a woodcock in a ditch which was a blind retrieve following every dog on the shooting field and their failed attempts. It had been in front of my best friends and she had filled my heart with pride. I had never seen a Labrador wag its tail more. After a few quiet moments I stood up and walk quietly back to the warmth of the house.

After a spot of lunch, a healthy chicken salad, I decided to switch the television on and sit down for a rest. My legs were very weak and my general fitness was staggeringly poor. I was extremely surprised at how quickly my fitness had deteriorated as a result of being bed bound. I switched on the digi box and scanned through the channels. As I flicked through I picked up the Parliament channel. Tony Blair was reporting to the common's liaison select committee and they were just starting to talk about the NHS. I was glued.

Tony Blair's performance to the Liaison committee suggested he was well informed and prepared to issue almost policy press statements as he talked. He appeared very relaxed and often joked with the MP's he sat before. He showed a depth of broad knowledge and talked openly and frankly about the issues across the departments of the government to his peers. I watched it avidly. With all of my recent experiences still fresh in my mind I was riveted to hear whether the politicians were in touch. There was no doubt that his style of almost casual, relaxed and at times light hearted debating with the various committee chairs was entertaining. It was also clear that this was a man on the way out and so there was bound to be a degree of nonchalance in comparison to 10 years ago. Nonetheless I was alarmed to find out that the chairman's questions and their follow ups by the Prime minister highlighted the depth of their knowledge and the lack of his. It further emphasised where his true interests lay. His answers on crime, the Home Office, and the criminal system were detailed and fleshed out. On almost everything else he was under par. In particular his answers on climate change and the NHS showed his lack of foresight and understanding of the enormous challenges we faced both as individuals and as a country. Phil Willis, the chair for Science and Technology asked him to explain what evidence there was to show an improvement in "the bottom up patient quality strategies". He was seeking an acceptance from the Prime minister that there wasn't any evidence. "Bottom up" means patient choice driving the improvements through the Health service. It means commercial decisions and consumer choice impacting upon the delivery of quality of service. It therefore needs people who recognise where the key indicators are, working in the Health service to drive the changes required to achieve the objectives. There is of course only a sparse contingent of these people and certainly no evidence in my experience of their existence and their impact upon the services of the NHS.

In response to Mr Willis' question the Prime minister recounted the governments' achievements on reducing waiting lists. The fact that patients could now choose which waiting list they wanted to attach themselves to, and so manage the decisions about when they received care, seemed to be a very important step forward for him. He rattled on about payment by results and the fact that the money will follow the patients. 'Hospitals hitting their targets will be more successful and receive more funding.' He talked about the importance of reducing the diagnostic wait for patients and how so very often this held up the process. He mentioned the shift from 95% to 98% of patients needing to be seen within 4 hours of admission to an A and E department. He discussed the evidence based last 3% proving very expensive to achieve. He made bold statements about the fact that A & E was significantly better than it was 10 years ago and that it represented the shop window of the NHS. I wished he'd been with me just over a week ago. I'd have loved to have talked to him about his 3%. He talked about appropriate care in appropriate settings; the increasing demand and expectations of an ageing population; the unnecessary treatment of certain patients who should not be in an

A & E department and the quicker turnaround times to discharge patients as soon as possible. He talked about how difficult it was to determine how to target funding. Central targeting for Cancer was clearly an important issue but there was doubt about local targeting. Nonetheless when he was asked as to whether patient choice should take over from central targeting from Richmond House, his reply was "Yes, this should happen. A free market should exist." He went on to state that financial incentives, patient choice and central targets working in combination should deliver the payment by results strategy. Willis cut in and stated that PCT's determined the choice and level of service available to patients and that the state dictated the budget and as a result, the patient had no real impact upon anything. Blair, funnily enough wasn't listening. He was more interested in talking further bollocks to defend his policies and his cabinet and his government. It all seemed an age away from the reality I had just experienced.

As I sat and watched his performance, his values and opinions stood in stark contrast to the reality on the ground. They talked in a stratosphere circling high above the reality of the NHS tornado which caused such catastrophe and disaster in people's lives way down below from the sight of his ivory tower. I was dismayed by the time Edward Leigh had started arguing the toss with the prime minister about the finer points of 'Discrimination trumping Conscience' as they debated about the human rights act, discrimination and there being a level playing field across the public, private and voluntary sectors of the health service. None of these issues were real when compared to cleaning Harold's bed or preventing MRSA or providing facilities and staffing in keeping with 2007. They were all contrived, political mumbo jumbo that did nothing to improve the standard of care the average patient in the NHS should be able to expect. It highlighted just how out of touch politicians really were. I turned it off. It was a depressing spectacle and I could feel a growing resentment and frustration that these people were so out of touch and so unprepared to deal with and debate the real issues.

I thought back through all of my brief and bitter experiences. The lack of support from my GP over the years in investigating my health issues; he had been aware that I was ill for some time and yet had never acted proactively to help resolve my health. I set great stall by him as I believed he was one of the good guys. But the health service and the system is one in which GPs only act reactively. They are spread thin and not motivated by the system to act in any other way. We as ill patients appear to be the only people who ultimately have any interest in repairing our health. NHS direct seemed a waste of time. I wondered just how many people had called it to be told to present themselves to A & E. I questioned how much it cost to have these qualified people directing traffic. The staff at the hospital on admissions whether they be receptionists, nurses or doctors were about as suited to be working in an A & E department as Josef Mengeler on a children's ward. I wondered whether Tony Blair had any idea that his wonderful vision of the NHS actually wasn't quite up to scratch. I would have loved to have seen his face when the staff all sat down to eat fish and chips. The facilities, protocols and systems on the ground didn't match any of the efficiencies he sat and suggested in front of his peers. There were clearly not enough beds, the ward system was archaic, the equipment needed updating and the medical staff needed retraining. The consultants were so detached or just chose to ignore the problems. They dehumanised the patients so that they could deal with the numbers. The care levels on the wards suggested understaffing and severe under performance particularly in the care of the elderly. Communication at almost every level seemed compromised almost all of the time. The irony was that the person with the best level of communication was a porter, who to be frank, used it too much. Beds were blocked up as a result of enormous inefficiency as people lay waiting to be seen for procedural examination. I would say at least 30% of the people I met could easily have been at home in bed or resting waiting to come in to be seen rather than laying wasting their and everybody else's time. The wards weren't clean, and the catering was sub standard for a care facility. Most of all I thought about the lady who cried as she was badgered by the staff most cruelly, the lady who called out throughout the nights, scared and alone and hardly ever attended, Barry in the hands of the people who had caused his present condiditon and suffering from a disease he would struggle with for the rest of his life, Harold laying in his own incontinence hour after hour and last but not least my grandfather who all of those years before had laid there at night scared and confused, knowing he was dying.

To see Tony Blair sat there crowing about his success and waxing lyrical about the NHS sickened me to the stomach.

Re-admission — a bad dream.

The next few days passed with enormous regularity. I sat alone pondering on all of the recent experiences. Apart from a few well wishers calling me on the phone and a visit from Anthony, a good pal, I was left to my own devices. I didn't feel great and no matter what I ate I constantly felt unwell. I called my GP a couple of times and tried to get some advice. I couldn't make my mind up as to whether the drugs I had been prescribed, omoprazole, were not agreeing with me or whether I was suffering from something new or these were the symptoms I should get used to as part of my condition. Would Crohn's do this to me forever? I so hoped it wasn't the latter. It seemed that the drugs were the likely cause but I needed to stay on them to make sure the course was completed. I didn't feel like eating much as I suffered constant nausea and occasional stomach ache. Over a period of a week I gradually worsened. Headaches, abdominal pain and increasing nausea led me to calling my GP again to find out whether he could see me. It was going to be three days before I could get an appointment. I was not happy. By the 31st January I felt bloody awful. Often confused, tired, de-motivated and in increasing pain I managed no sleep at all through the proceeding night. That morning as I writhed under the duvet clutching my stomach I managed to call the emergency number for my GP to lever myself up as a priority. I also called in the cavalry and spoke to Mum again. She was clearly concerned and promised to keep in touch regularly whilst we found out what my GP was going to do. He called me back and promised to make a home visit later in the day. He would be with me as soon as possible but thought it would be about mid day. It was a great relief and I felt enormously reassured that he would be with me sooner than later. I knew I was getting worse. The pain was becoming very intense and the rest of the morning became a blur. I lay weakened and contorted in so much pain that I couldn't speak. I screwed my face up as the pain came in waves. It hurt so much I felt tears running down my face as the agony racked up the pressure on my control systems. It felt like I was heading for another disaster and I was becoming scared of a reoccurrence and all of the associated recent experiences which would come with it. It had been such a relief to escape hospital and now the way things were going it seemed apparent that I might be heading back in. I was determined to not make the same mistake as I had before and rely on admission through the general hospital. I wanted to try and make sure I was going to receive a standard of care I felt comfortable with. As my condition worsened Mum arrived and through gritted teeth I tried to rationalise my concerns to her. Like a broody hen there was some feather fluffing and scampering around with concern as her offspring appeared seriously ill. On the phone in a flash she called the private hospital to try to admit me but they were unwilling to accept me without either a consultant's or my health scheme's approval. The Health scheme wouldn't sanction my admittance without the consultants say so. As mum tried to contact the consultants it became clear that they were all at the funeral of another local and very eminent consultant who had only recently passed away. Mum and Dad would have been at the funeral themselves but for my untimely demise. None of the consultants would be available for some time.

A mild panic set in as it looked more and more like the general hospital would be the only solution. I was however indignant that death in my own bedroom was a considerably happier outcome than reliance upon some fish and chip eating, coke guzzling, vending machine vandal who would park me in an open space in the middle of A & E. There was no way I was going back in to the general hospital. Mum reluctantly began leaving messages on mobile answer phones. Eventually someone would look at their messages and maybe be able to do something for me.

After an agonising half an hour for my parents who felt utterly helpless as they watched me writhe around in pain my GP arrived. As ever his calm approach and concern lent considerable reality to the circus which had started to result in my bedroom. He felt my abdomen, checked my vitals and looked at various bits of me. "Sorry Ed I need to admit you. I'm not quite sure what's going on right now but there's nothing I can do for you here. Ok? I need you in a hospital ASAP. Do you want me to call an ambulance or are your parents going to take you in?" Through gritted teeth and short painful breaths I explained that I preferred the concept of agonising death to going back into the general hospital. He understood. He departed the bedroom and went to parley with the parents. I could hear the problems being explained to him. He thought it through and decided to call the Health scheme company and private hospital himself to sanction my admittance. The health scheme still wouldn't allow my admission to a private hospital; somewhere a minion on the end of a telephone with insufficient clout was holding up my treatment. Unless a consultant approved and arranged my admittance I wasn't going in. My GP promised to keep trying to arrange things as he left and promised to keep in touch. I lay firmly in my pit resisting the growing pressure to choose the general hospital. It really was going to be over my dead body.

Eventually Mum received a message from Chris. He advised setting off immediately to the hospital and somehow he would make sure everything was clear for my admission. It was a great relief. I crawled out of bed and bent double in pain did my best to dress myself sufficiently to lend modesty to my public arrival at the hospital. I was steered downstairs, back out of the house I had so enjoyed coming home to only so recently, and fell onto the back seat of my parent's car in mortal agony. The makeshift ambulance set off.

Somewhere between home and the hospital Chris and his wife were working miracles and eventually they called to say that the way was clear. They had leaned on the health scheme's administrators. Even with their clout, they had found it difficult to arrange admittance as the minion on the phone had requested that specific procedures needed to be met. Only confirmation of the reason for my admission, what my health problems were, and what procedures I would be undergoing whilst admitted would allow the process of my admission to be sanctioned. Eventually Chris had told them that I would be undergoing several tests and that I was extremely ill and needed immediate care. Once he had scared them sufficiently he had called the hospital and made sure a room was available for me. To this day I cannot tell you how relieved and grateful I was to them for arranging everything. Their kindness, commitment, determination and ability shone through like a standard bright in the sun on a battle field. I felt so ill at the time I was way beyond arranging anything for myself and dependent upon people who genuinely cared about me to make sure I was well looked after. If all of the consultants in the health service believed in the patient as much as Chris did, it would be a service which was far more capable and effective and an organisation with genuine worldwide credibility. He understands the fear of illness and people's concerns. He appreciates we all have important lives to lead and how quickly we need to recover and he relates to you as both a human being and a customer whilst providing you with both dignity and respect. Over my time in hospital and through the course of the next few weeks I learnt that consultants have a choice about how they behave, what they say and how they treat you as a patient. How they talk to you, how they communicate all of the medical information we are not trained to either understand or appreciate. It's a skill which some have and others do not. It's an important part of their role. As a patient you need to be well informed and kept up to date with what's happening to you. Chris was excellent at doing this. He was also a great practitioner, old school perhaps, but nonetheless fully behind the belief in his abilities and aware of how frustrating many of the methods and systems which exist in the health service are today. Whilst I eventually remained under Con 2 who agreed to see me in the private hospital it was Chris who constantly gave me the confidence to both understand what was happening to me and to see a potentially happy outcome to it all. I will forever remain in his debt.

Once I arrived at the hospital I was quickly processed and allocated a room. Still in considerable pain and clutching my stomach ineffectively I was nonetheless delighted to meet a South African registrar who began the twenty questions lark again. This time it was different. Although a lot of the content we covered was over the same ground the questions were now interspersed with leading open questions and very often we went down alleys and lanes of my medical history to ascertain as clear a picture as possible. I had brought in various old drug cartons dating back from the dreaded anti inflammatory drugs through to the omoprazole I had taken to date. He was interested as had been the last doctor I had seen at the general hospital in the sequence of events leading up to my initial bleed. He struggled however to explain what was going on right now. I was administered some pain relief, put on a drip and had all of my vital signs checked. The main ones seemed ok. Chris arrived and after a reassuring 5 minutes he arranged various tests for me to undergo. X rays and an ultrasound were set up for the morning. A sister arrived and took swabs from my groin, nose and throat which were to be sent off for analysis to check for MRSA and everyone wore gowns in and out of the room whilst they remained unsure of my condition. The hand cleansers were adopted each time anyone entered or left the room. A sense of cleanliness and measured efficient routine cloaked the facilities. The place reeked of organisation and competent procedures. Every 30 minutes a nurse would poke her head around the door and check I was ok. When the light failed and night started to chase the shadows across the room, a nurse popped in and turned on a light and checked I was ok again. Although I was extremely concerned about my condition I felt reassured by my surroundings. As the pain relief kicked in I found myself relaxing. Since I had not slept for 36 hours I felt absolutely shattered. My abdomen whilst still painful was now manageable and as evening kicked in I slipped in to the land of nod.

I woke up with a start. I felt confused and my brain didn't seem to be working. I started to focus and realised I was moving. A light in the ceiling looked strange and unfamiliar. As I came to, I realised I was in an ambulance. My mind raced. How? Why? I tried to lift my head and a paramedic appeared by my side. "Hi, you're awake. Good. Nothing to worry about! Soon have you there." I was full of questions, suddenly terrified, but I couldn't bring myself to speak. I felt terribly ill. Nausea gripped me but I was too confused to register whether it was because of my illness or just fear. I had a drip attached and an ECG monitoring my output. The ambulance began swerving as it rounded tight corners repeatedly at speed and then it abruptly stopped and began reversing. The doors opened and the two paramedics set up my trolley and wheeled me out of the ambulance. I was back at the general. Panic overtook me and I tried to lift myself off the bed. "It's ok. Don't worry. We'll soon have you there." The trouble was I didn't want to be there and I didn't know what was going on. "What's happening?" I managed to speak but my voice sounded weak and croaky. "Let's get you up to theatre. Everything will be sorted. Don't worry." I was completely out of control, terrified and desperately lonely. I was unsure of what was going on and no one appeared to tell me a thing. As corridor lights flashed overhead and doors crashed open and shut as we passed through them at pace I could feel myself drifting back again, to a safe place. My last memories of the corridors were the full dustbins and the peeling paint.

I don't know how long I had been out but as I came round and my eyes adjusted to the gloom I could see a familiar ceiling above me. I could hear noises all around me. A Nurse was administering to another patient further down the ward. I was back on the same ward as I had departed only a week or so ago. My first reaction was to run away as quickly as possible. I tried to get up but was too weak to move. Fear gripped me. I could hear moaning and disturbed breathing from the other patients. I looked around. The dustbins were overflowing, dirty cups sat about the tables on the ends of the beds. A bed bath was being conducted a bay down from me. It was hell. I called out and all that emitted from my dry and crispy lips was a moan. The male nurse conducting the bed bath appeared wearing gloves and apron. You could smell the other patient on him. "What am I doing here?" I managed to force the question out, but it was barely a whisper. "You have MRSA. You are very ill. You all have MRSA. Rest now. Someone will be here to see you shortly." "What about the others? Barry, Pete, George, Harold?" I rasped. "All gone I'm afraid. They didn't make it." My mind couldn't take it in. "What?" "They all died of MRSA, sorry."

I sat bolt upright in bed. I was covered in sheens of sweat and my heart raced. I couldn't breathe properly and I felt as though a great weight hung around my neck. I tried breathing in and nothing happened. I coughed violently and suddenly air surged into my lungs. Wide eyed I looked around the room searching for a reference. There sat on the chair next to my bed were the clothes I had been wearing when I had been admitted to the single room I lay in within the private hospital. I had suffered nothing more than a terribly realistic nightmare, one that reflected my greatest fear. One that most disconcertedly, could so easily have been true.

It had seemed so real. I immediately began gathering my thoughts and realised just how scared I had been. I could feel the sweat running down my neck. The relief I felt as my surroundings conquered the nightmare and my reality became evident was enormous. It felt like a silly dream within minutes but then it had seemed so real that it made me think that it was all so feasible too. The general had suffered an outbreak of a superbug in the recent past and to be caught up in it must have been an absolute nightmare for patients and families alike. I had seen more precautions in half a day in this hospital than I saw in the entire time I was in the general. Whilst it had only been a dream, somewhere in my brain there had been a momentary fix of a false reality which felt utterly terrifying. My thoughts drifted to all of the people who suffer this avoidable and indignant end to their lives and I felt utter relief I wasn't one of them. I drifted for a while, not asleep, not awake. I was so unsettled by the experience I was frightened of sleeping in case I repeated the dream or had some sort of panic attack. I switched on the TV, which I didn't have to pay for and with the volume set low, I skipped through the channels until my eyelids became heavy and my reactions slower. After a while tiredness overtook me and I finally fell back into an undisturbed sleep.

Morning arrived with a thread of light forcing itself through a chink in the curtains. From my bed I could see a garden outside my window. It was a happy view. As I stirred I could feel my troublesome guts and their related discomfort. Back to nil by mouth I was feeling weak, but slightly less tired. The pain wasn't as full on as the day before and I felt slightly more in control as a result. At about 8am a sister came in to see me and explained that I would be off for x ray and then an ultra sound scan. Within 30 minutes another younger nurse arrived and dutifully helped me into a hospital dressing gown, put me in a wheel chair and pushed me around to the x ray department. They were kind, considerate, chatty and very human. It took about 15 minutes to be x rayed and then a further half an hour to be scanned. I had to sit and wait for about half an hour for my scan whilst a few out patients fitted their appointments in before me. I sat on a settee reading the paper and occasionally grimaced as the pain ebbed and flowed. It was considerably more comfortable than where I had been before and at little extra expense. A comfy sofa, nice decor, a few smiles and a communal paper to read made all of the difference.

By the time I had been back in my bed for a couple of hours, Con 2 arrived. As fate would have it I was meant to have seen him anyway as it had been the date of my first consultation since my discharge from the general. I thought I had done really well to minimise the disruption to his diary by falling ill on the very day I was booked in to see him, but

I didn't get the impression he was that pleased to see me. I got the feeling I had let the side down being admitted to a private hospital; clearly not the done thing! I noticed he neither wore any gloves or an apron nor washed his hands with the antiseptic dispenser. It was clearly a cultural NHS thing. After a few initial pleasantries he suggested that the results from my tests would possibly lend some clarity to my present position. He decided to examine me and tried to adjust the bed. The side guards were up and he attempted to lower them. He fiddled with various controls on the bed without success and extraordinarily exclaimed, "Typical private hospital equipment, too complicated and expensive. Lot easier on the NHS!" I was amazed that he would be so unprofessional and make such a slighted comment. He carried on as though he had said nothing at all and began his examination. He found some discomfort on my right side which he explained supported the Crohn's theory but it could also be other conditions as well. I hoped he was wrong about the crohns. Once he had lent nothing more to my well being, or my state of mind about his abilities, he suggested that he would be back later, report back on the test results and then determine what course of action to take. I couldn't wait. The pain had subsided a little and along with the continuing pain relief I was despite not eating, feeling better than I had for several days.

My day wore on watching TV and reading. Mum popped in to see me for a short visit and to catch up with all of the medical news. Neither of us could quite get our heads round the lack of progress made on determining what was causing me to be ill. There didn't seem to be any urgency from Con 2 in diagnosing the condition or determining my treatment. I just wanted to get better. It was incredibly frustrating. On the plus side I was as comfortable as I could be, I had my own personal bathroom facilities, the staff were attentive and kind and I generally felt a little bit better.

At about six o'clock Con 2 knocked on my door and came in. "Right got the results. The x ray showed a blockage, probably caused by a stricture on the right side near the end of the ileum and the scan showed normal liver, kidneys, bladder etc. but quite a lot of inflammation generally in your bowel. It ties up with the discomfort I have noticed on your right side whenever I examine you." "What's causing it?" I asked. "Can't tell you but it's not cancer, OK?" He glared at me as though I was some sort of spoilt school child. I looked blankly back at him. "Ok?" he repeated, "You understand you haven't got cancer? You should be pleased!" I was of course pleased and I wondered whether he had muddled me up with another patient as I had never discussed such an issue with him before. I had never considered I had cancer and rather hoped no one else thought I had either. I suddenly thought about all of the poor souls who do get the bad news from him. I wasn't sure whether I was getting a sudden grilling because he had decided I was a malingerer now wasting private medical health resources or because he was fed up because Chris had been involved in arranging my tests which had taken less than a day to undergo and receive the results, when in the NHS it took a week to achieve the equivalent action. I couldn't understand his attitude. He continued to glare at me, so I glared back. I certainly wasn't pleased as I still didn't know what it actually was. Seconds felt like minutes as I matched his gaze in a wilful attempt to gain the upper hand over his stare. Eventually I broke the silence still staring into his glinting pupils, "I have never believed I had cancer. It was not something I had considered. Surely some of the analyses from the colonoscopy would have pointed to that. I am particularly hacked off however with having been ill on and off for nearly twenty years, never being diagnosed, never knowing what might be wrong with me, never knowing how to manage my health and everyone always taking a dim view of me whenever I might feel a bit unwell because it appears I'm whinging again. You've had me in a hospital for two weeks on and off , I've seen lots of different doctors and undergone several tests and yet I neither really know what's the matter with me or how long I'm going to remain unwell. I know I haven't got cancer. I'm probably not an urgent case in your opinion, but I still don't feel very bloody well and I would like to find out what the hell is the matter with me! I would very much like your opinion on what is wrong with me and how long I can expect to be in hospital and what is likely to happen to me now. Ever since I've been on those omoprazole I've felt crap. Are they the cause? I do have a life to lead and it would be nice to be able to explain to the people I live my life with, what I am doing and what is likely to happen to me. I would hope that that wasn't too much to ask!" My voice rose to such a volume that it finished in a crescendo. From somewhere deep inside a subdued anger had surfaced and then erupted like a volcano. The silence that followed was not untypical to what one might experience on the top of a mountain on a very clear still morning. It was a deafening silence. I still held his stare.

Eventually he looked away and I felt some sort of moral victory had been achieved. I could tell I had taken him by surprise. Something changed in his attitude. He softened a little and put his hands together in front of his body in a submissive gesture. His voice was conciliatory, "Look, right now we just can't be sure what it is. It could be one of several things, it could have been the drugs you took in November, it could be the omoprazole now, it could be crohn's it could have been an infection; erm we found ulceration in the ileum, didn't we?" He looked at me requiring confirmation. I nodded, "That's right." I was suddenly a bit concerned that he couldn't remember. "Yes, that's right we found it high up. Even so we just can't be absolutely sure. We need to do more tests before deciding which course of action to take. If it is Crohns and if we find chronic and acute symptoms, fissures, fistulas, more ulceration it could mean surgery. But it's a last gasp that one. Before then there are various drug treatments we can rely on, immunosuppresants, steroids, that kind of thing. To get to the point where we can make sure we need to do a more intimate analyses of the bowel using a camera capsule or an MRI. First of all I would like to do a barium x ray examination. I'm cautious of the capsule because of its potential complications." I was amazed. He had never so openly discussed the options and I felt that just because I had been firm with a raised voice and I had demanded information he had complied. "When can I have the x ray done?" "Well I just don't know. Could be a few weeks." Having been successful once, I bristled again, "That's not good enough. Could I have it sooner?" "Er, well the general can't just fit you in, it will depend on what their work load is." "Not good enough, if they can't do it find me a hospital that can. I can't believe there isn't an x ray department somewhere within a 100 mile radius that wouldn't accept me and conduct the test. It's bloody ridiculous. We are not living in a third world country!" "Mmm, I like working with people I know at the general" countered Con2. "Please can you find out and let me know." He appeared as though he was tiring of my persistent approach and fell silent. "When can I go home or do I have to wait here indefinitely?" "If your bowel habits are normal, you feel well enough and all of your obs are ok I think sometime tomorrow or the day after." With that he asked whether I had any more questions and since I had run out and appeared on the edge of exploding he said his goodbyes and left me to my rather hot room. If anyone checked either my temperature or blood pressure in the next half an hour I wouldn't be going home for a week.

I in fact spent a further 36 hours in hospital before both consultants and nursing staff alike were happy for me to go home. They were not on their own. I was delighted that my most recent trip in to hospital had turned into a minor event. Eventually the pain had completely subsided, everything including my regularly discussed bowel habits became normal again and I felt reasonably well despite not being fed for three days. I was picked up and taken home by a member of staff who worked on the farm. I didn't mind it not being someone closer to home and it was good to catch up with what had been going on in the business and he was interested to hear what had been happening to me as his mother had recently undergone a similar experience with a similar outcome with the same consultant. He was not alone. Over the space of the next few weeks I was amazed by the number of people who told me about their experience. It always sounded so familiar whenever they recounted their stories. I started wondering whether I should put pen to paper and tell my story.

Within a week I got my barium x ray at the general arranged by Con 2. I sat in a public seating area in the general hospital wearing nothing other than a hospital gown, waiting to be seen having been told to change in to the gown some thirty minutes earlier. I constantly tried to maintain and protect my modesty from the crowd who sat around me waiting for their x rays too. Strangely they all remained clothed. I was first up. I clenched my knees tightly together and tried to keep elbow contact with my neighbours to a minimum. I couldn't believe out of twenty people I was the only one sat half naked in the room. I couldn't help but laugh at the situation I found myself in nor at the comments I listened to from amongst my fellow out patients. Next to me a middle aged lady watching the

TV, which was provided high on its shelf, commented to all and sundry that she'd used some of that self tanning stuff Lorraine Kelly was advising her audience to use. "Goes dead streaky and it sends your hands brown too". Another couple to my left and in front of me were having a strange conversation which at least distracted me from the feeling of a light breeze on my nether regions. "That sign, I can't read it on that notice board. It's wrong that sign isn't it?" I tried to look at the notice board to gain some insight in to her issue with the sign. "Which one love" her partner enquired. "That bright yellow one, it's doing my head in. Who makes a bright yellow sign? It's a health and safety hazard. I can't stop looking at it. Oh, my eyes. It's so bright." "Yeah see what you mean love, black would be loads better." "Or blue maybe, a dull red, but not yellow." I shook my head and closed my eyes and wished the earth would open beneath me or at least a nurse would appear and ask for me. I wondered where the inspiration came from for the nursing profession to deal with people. Eventually my prayers were answered and I was led into a room with a large examination table surrounded by x ray equipment. As I scuttled into the x ray department I had to cling to my gown at the rear to avoid a 'Full Monty' show to my prospective audience. Even so I could hear a titter from row 3 which I was convinced had something to do with my awkward shuffle towards the door. Inside the department everyone wore bullet proof jackets to restrict themselves from the impending radiation. Everyone of course except me, who was about to be exposed to Chernobyl. They explained that I would have to have a tube shoved up my nose the width of a straw and down into my stomach. I looked at them sceptically as I had never had anything up my nose beyond the length of my little finger and a catkin which lodged itself up there at the age of 4. They sprayed a local anaesthetic up my nose and proceeded to work the tube in.

After about two inches it came to a dead stop. No matter how they pushed, twisted or slid the thing in, it wouldn't go. I was dancing all over the place like a cat on a hot tin roof. There was no way it was going to happen. Staff kept trying to hold my head steady and my arms by my side but I just kept saying "No, No, NO!" After several abortive attempts they suggested I swallow it. Have you ever tried to swallow a tube, stone cold sober without any lubrication? Well don't! It was impossible. After a further ten minutes of valuable NHS time had evaporated and I was no nearer to absorbing any barium the nurse suggested I drink it. What a sensible suggestion and in the space of about 10 seconds I had consumed all of the barium required. It resembled white paste and tasted of metal. I could feel it drifting through my body which as time progressed became less of a drift and more of a hot torrent. The timing for the x rays and me erupting with barium was indeed a finely tuned operation which left only seconds from an embarrassing predicament and a lot of cleaning. Within an hour it was all over and the whole procedure showed a normal bowel with nothing to see.

Within two weeks I had been down to London for a specialist MRI examination using a contrasting dye in my blood to lend definition to the images shown up on the scan. The consultant in charge had an unrivalled reputation for excellence in his field. A few symptoms of Crohns including narrowing and inflammation were picked up on the scan as well as a metal shard which tried to erupt from my finger in an alien/John Hurt sort of moment which was surreal. Con 2 had arranged the test and sought out the eminent specialist in good time and I was duly impressed. I still felt that by shouting louder I had finally received the attention I deserved. When I met him again periodically over the next few months he displayed a far more professional approach and he openly talked to me about my condition in infinite medical detail. I felt as though he was finally treating me as an equal. He wanted me to go onto a course of immuno-suppressant drugs, asothioprin to be exact, which would counter the crohns. However he didn't force the decision upon me but wisely allowed me a month to think about it.

I thought about it and came to the decision that I didn't like the idea of suppressing your immune system and becoming reliant upon a course of drugs which might not be sustainable in the long term anyway. I talked to numerous people including my GP about the implications of being dependent on a quite aggressive drugs regime. I formed my own opinions and instead selected a course of less intrusive improvements to my life style. I increased my fitness levels by going to the gym three times a week, changed my diet based on some food allergy tests I had done, started taking fish oil and more importantly a daily probiotic containing 16 billion friendly bacteria. The results were astonishing and finally after twenty years I seemed to get on top of a condition that had plagued me most of my adult life. Whenever I met Con 2 for a consultation he listened to the choices I had made, considered my opinions and ideas and actually agreed with my course of action. In combination with his continuing observations of my health, his support in my decisions to not take the drugs and his continuing help on an ongoing basis has given me the confidence to take my care into my own hands and have the confidence to make appropriate decisions about my health. I feel 100% better and whilst it is very early days I feel confident that my health is on the mend. My opinion of him now is that he has finally come good and that he has provided a very well informed and thoroughly eminent level of advice. He took his time about it though. Even so, including Con 2, no one can fully explain to this day what caused the onset of my acute bleed.

When anyone asks me what the difference is to my health now and when I fell ill, I can safely say that I look after myself, now knowing that I need to. I eat better food, have a healthier diet, take more regular exercise, take more care of my general health, take fish oil daily and rely on probiotics to establish healthy bacteria in my gut. Whilst it's not proven, a lot of work has been done in establishing the benefits they bring to inflammatory bowel disease. I used to think I looked after myself pretty well before but sometimes it's just about understanding what's right for you. Knowing what is wrong with you is half the battle. Getting people to listen to you is a big part of getting the right treatment. Putting yourself first becomes essential. Of course I was lucky. I could shout loud. I learnt throughout my experience that so many cannot and for them I remain extremely concerned.

Prognosis and cures.

My story is probably quite typical and I know from talking to dozens of people before, during and after my time in hospital that many have experienced unhappy times being looked after by the NHS. Someone asked me, when I explained that I wanted to write an account of what I went through - Why? What are you trying to achieve? It was a very good question. I was of course quite angry about the many encounters I experienced. But I also realised that many people would have been through the same thing and not known whether they were right to feel indignant themselves. Should one say anything or should you keep your head down? I hoped by writing my account it would inform people and perhaps give them the confidence to talk about their experiences too. The more your local MP knows the better. Let's face it this government pretty much got rid of the patient's charter and any right to complain about anything so it's good to have a chance to express your views. What's more, it was a cathartic experience and I found that mental well being was an important contribution to overall recovery. Furthermore I knew that some people would have been through inflammatory bowel disease issues and would have been scared and embarrassed by the condition. I wanted to let people know that through the struggle and the fear there was another side and that they weren't on their own. When you realise that there is a cure and there are people who can help, it is very comforting. Be aware however, they take some finding and it can be a very long road. Very often the advice is confusing and contradictory. Inflammatory bowel disease is not a black and white illness and everyone's experience is different. What works for one isn't forced to be right for the next. It would have been considerably more difficult without the internet and a realisation that I had as much chance of figuring out how to resolve my health issues as some of the medical personnel before me. Looking back they helped establish what was wrong but they were vague about how to put it right. It has taken me many years to finally find a solution when I look back. I remain very frustrated that in the past people haven't advised me better. I suspect I could have reached a healthier conclusion sooner with the right advice. Whatever your experience, do try and keep smiling, although I know it's bloody difficult at times. The health service is occasionally funny, although it also makes you want to cry too. It certainly makes you think. Apart from just telling my story I wanted to contribute to the debate on the NHS and highlight some of the stark realities patients on wards suffer with every day. It's wrong and it needs to change. In addition I wanted in my own small way to be able to make a contribution to improving the NHS or at least in some small way help funding some of its work in the area of inflammatory bowel disease. As such a contribution goes to the National Association for Colitis and Crohn's Disease each time someone buys a copy of this book. I suppose I have achieved at least one aim. I finally wanted to draw sufficient attention to my story to lend a platform to enable discussion in a few of the areas which do in my opinion need urgent reassessment in the NHS.

As the pressure mounts on the NHS, there is a greater chance that as each of us becomes reliant upon it at some point in our lives, to preserve and improve our health, we will be tragically disappointed. An ageing and growing population levers more and more demands upon an archaic structure. For example, the immigration policy in New Zealand supports the concept of only allowing immigrants and eventual citizenship on the basis that they will not add a net cost to the economy. In other words if you are old or ill you are less likely to be allowed in. If you can earn money which contributes to the turnover of the economy and at the same time lend little cost to the state you will be more likely to gain entry. The pressures that a growing population here in the UK brings to its national health service, particularly at a time when less earners and thus less tax payers as a percentage of the population are available to support it, indicates trouble ahead. Liberal political decisions and a lack of measures relating to population control need to be addressed soon. We cannot go on handing out. Each British citizen, old, young or recent deserves a quality of service and fairness for the contribution they make to the state.

We have an ageing population and the retirement age is being put back to try and address the issues created by the reliance upon dozens of societies services including some within the NHS. The problem is that moving the retirement age makes no difference to our health. Nature takes its course. We get old and eventually ill as our bodies decay. When you are in hospital the one thing you notice is the majority of beds which are taken up in the general wards by the elderly. Unless R & D come up with some wonder drug which maintains our health up to the point of death we are going to require more and more care facilities within the NHS. The problem, obvious enough, is that an ever greater reliance is going to be placed upon those still fit enough to work and therefore earn to support those who cannot. I know I will find this a distinctly difficult concept as I continue to pay my taxes, despite my recent dependence upon the health service, particularly when I know that money is being wasted, mis-used and badly managed. This really is one of the most important issues the government has to face in managing the NHS resources. Quite rightly the nation's health is an important aspect to the problem. We need to look after ourselves, eat better, keep fitter and minimise our dependency upon the health service. We need to make adequate provision for our old age including not just our retirement, but also our health and care management. There needs to be greater resources deployed to care management for the elderly by government. We need to put policies in place which gear themselves to meeting the requirements of a rising elderly population. We need to re emphasise the contribution that the elderly have made in their lives to our country and economy and make sure that the services provided for them deliver a service which reflects the dignity with which they should be served. It is a sad reflection on our society and our health service that the Harolds of this world and the lady who cried out but never received any attention are treated in this way. As a country we need to decide how important our elderly citizens are. Let's face it we all become one eventually.

The NHS is as much a social as an economic dilemma. You can feel an undercurrent of 'New Labour' and their political correctness gone mad. At the same time one can recognise the old true left wing principles engrained in the philosophies and systems established by Atlee and Bevan which many of the personnel abide by. It used to be about serving the people, but the focus has been lost, and now it seems to be about people's rights, not least those that work within it. The staff cling to making sure their own interests are met as a result of an everyday risk of over burdening litigation and the fact that our working population want more money for less work. Very often the patient is the last thing they think about. Form filling, meeting initiatives, following protocols and hitting targets become the focus of so many hospital departments. On top of that my experience showed me that there is a ridiculous undercurrent of competition between the private sector and the NHS. The NHS personnel have a chip on their shoulder about the private sector and yet 1 in 6 people in the UK have some form of private medical insurance. It's not an elitist club! However in return and I guess as a reaction the private sector dangerously spends a bit too much time looking down its nose at the NHS. It's an absurd situation as both sectors of the health service should be working together to achieve the common goal, curing patients. I am of course generalising here and there are many excellent hospitals, departments and personnel in each sector who between them have enabled life saving care for thousands of people over the years who would probably want nothing bad said about the infrastructures that saved their lives either. Unfortunately that level of care is not evenly distributed across the services and it is of course not as simple as that. Serving society is a vocation as important as any, we as human beings, can follow. Whether you work in the health service, work in other emergency services, work in law, the civil service, government, teach or even grow food as a farmer you are all serving the greater good in what you do or produce. We, of course, all take our personal share of the pie in our pay or profit; what we consider to be due to us for our contribution. Unfortunately for so many of us this has become our main motivation for whatever vocation we follow. Money unfortunately rules our lives and in our present economy so many of us find ourselves under financial pressures which just didn't exist forty years ago. Many of the nursing staff will go to work thinking about when they will get paid, how they will cover their mortgage, what time they will get off work, and whether the kids will be ok at school today. More time will be wasted at work filling in forms, shuffling paper, double checking risk assessments and offloading responsibility to lighten the case book. Time is often taken up tittle tattling about what was said to who about cock up number 1,2 or 3 as each person tries to admonish themselves from the blame culture they live and work in. The patient, the job, and the care requirements will fill the remaining time but not necessarily as a priority to the many other issues we choose to consider as important in our working lives. Not many doctors and nurses will come to work with their headlights switched on full beam and concentrate on the health and patient and customer issues before them from the moment they step into the hospital. It is an essential requirement that patients are considered as customers and that despite all of the complexities that these consumers bring to the everyday activities in a hospital they are regarded as such. Being target driven is important of course. We all need something to head for; our key performance indicators. As the business consultants say, if you can't measure it, you can't manage it. The problem is that government sets the targets and usually they are fiscally or politically motivated. They are rarely patient driven. Unless there is a turn round in the way the performance of the NHS is measured it will never achieve the enormous task before it. Reducing waiting lists is all well and good as long as the figures stack up and the system hasn't been manipulated by the PCT's to earn money. Similarly paying doctors for doing more work has some merit to it until you find out all they have to do is conduct a simple examination and then fill a form in to get the money. The KPI's need to be about curing people, and making people healthy again, as efficiently as possible. The focus has to go back to patient care and it has to be set up in a way that it can't be diminished by those it's trying to inspire. The standard of care, the efficiency of the use of the resource in healing the patient, the welfare of the patient and the value for money each successful outcome is achieved in are the type of top down measures we should be pursuing. The problem with pursuing reduction in waiting times for investigatory procedures, for example, is that staff are almost expected to cut corners to achieve output. If you can guarantee funding by achieving targets which are based on pushing numbers through the system, you can bet your last dollar that policies are not going to be focused on quality. This can lead to things getting missed which eventually cost money. One of the big problems is the spin that is thrown around the headline issues that the NHS generates in its confused contradictory search for acclaim. Political headlines are always twisting reality. No one can forget Patricia Hewitt declaring that reducing bed numbers and closing hospitals was an indication of the efficiencies of the NHS. The politicians and this government in particular have a lot to answer for. They have not despite their many claims benefited the NHS for the long term. Too much time has been spent on political point scoring and investing in high profile policy changes which the Government hopes brings them commendation and notoriety. Not enough time has been spent on managing the resources which were available to improve the service. Some of this does fall beyond the politicians control and within the domain of the civil service. I know from my own bitter experiences with the Rural Payments Agency which for the last three years has been responsible for handling the new payment system post reform of the Common Agricultural Policy that incompetence exists at every level. In this case the government and the ministers in charge at the time, created an over complicated and burdensome process. They massively underestimated the amount of paperwork, management, administration and mapping of the UK which would be needed to determine the allocation of the payment based on their system. There was advice available within the industry to counter the measures the government was pursuing at the time, but no one wanted to listen. It has cost millions of tax payer's additional pounds to deal with the horrendous foul ups which have subsequently been caused by the poor initial planning. No other country managing the same payment throughout Europe undertook such a complicated procedure and funnily enough no other European country has any problems which match ours. The UK RPA is still sorting out the 2005 payment, never mind the 2007. The indications are that the same badly thought out administration straps the NHS and when you see the debacle and extra cost trying to implement a new IT system in the health service and the problems it has caused it makes you wonder who the hell is making any decisions within the management of the resources of our country.

Of course nothing can be achieved without money, good or bad. Investment in the NHS is a prerequisite. The problem is that this recent government has spent an enormous amount of money on the NHS already and not really achieved much with it. We have wasted an opportunity. The clear and present danger is that they are still doing it, day after day. Again the ridiculous cost of implementing the new IT system is symptomatic of the problem. I can quite honestly say that the last thing on any of the people's minds that I shared hospital space with during my illness was IT. I am of course not so narrow minded as to dismiss investment in IT. It is the future after all. However a tiny proportion of the over spend alone would contribute such significant improvements in so many different departments of our local NHS hospital that people would appreciate it way beyond any perceived benefit from connectivity. Let's face it a consultant's secretary can call up a GP's surgery for notes; it's neither complicated nor expensive. But we still can't keep MRSA out of our hospitals, we still have mixed wards and under par A&E units, we still can't come up with enough staff at weekends, we still feed patients sub standard diets, we still can't find the money to replace old equipment, we still haven't enough money to invest in improving patient facilities and we clearly do not have staff that are sufficiently well trained operating in our hospitals. More ludicrous still, the government and the PCTs are busy closing wards and hospitals. It's plainly ridiculous. It makes one wonder who prioritises the budget spends. Who is truly accountable in the system?

Even if it is possible for someone to tighten their hold on the purse strings you still need good resource management. You need people who can allocate funding in hospitals into areas which can make a significant difference to both patient care and staff facilities. Yet without leadership in the hospitals the money will be wasted. I don't mean down the drain wasted, I'm talking about missed opportunities and underutilization. It became clear to me that within the heart of the hospital I experienced in the NHS there was a deep cultural rut which needed shaking out. There was a "don't care" undertow which had to come from the top. For staff to behave in the way they did, for people to show so little responsibility at times in an environment when life itself was at stake, something must be very wrong with the philosophy of those who led them. I admit we are all accountable and each person needs to carry their load in order for a team to succeed, the weakest link and all that. Even so when quality training isn't there, if personal development is lacking, whilst no one cares about the state of the environment and people have forgotten why they come to work other than the fact it's a job, there is bound to be under performance. Whether it's nurses, radiologists, porters, cleaners, kitchen staff, junior doctors, or even the more powerful consultants and managers, without a vision and some sharp focus to the vision, people cannot work together to achieve their goals. Strong leadership combined with a clear vision delivers for organisations. People need something to focus on and they need someone to inspire them towards it. The NHS is short of both.

The NHS is like every other organisation in the UK. It's not special. It depends on people, just like every other business large or small. Who those people are, whether they feel valued, how well trained they are, the management above them and the environment in which they work all determine their effectiveness. The problem for the NHS which is unique is that it has such an enormous challenge in front of it and those people are the ones who every day have to face that challenge. The challenge is unique simply because of its enormity. Whether it be the scale of the organisation, the difficulties associated with communication, the vast range of departments, the unequivocal strain on resources whether it be drugs, labour or IT, the huge human resources issues, the limitless technologies or just the fact that every day a new wave of ill people arrive at your door when you are already overloaded, it is not difficult to appreciate the huge contribution required from all of those who work in the NHS. What defies logic however is that when so much is at stake the system fails the people. I am not well enough informed to know where the boundaries of responsibility are between politicians, civil servants, PCT managers and consultants. What I do know is that until they sort out between them a better structure for dealing with the organisation than the one they have, they will not succeed. We urgently need investment in the infrastructure of our hospitals. We need modern clean facilities. We must have new thinking within the design and ideas of hospital management. Wards are not an efficient way of managing patients. We need R&D and technological advancement but primarily within the basic care facilities and operating facilities of the hospitals. Not in the offices and administration departments although I am sure improvements could be made with a limited budget and some inspired thinking.

This is important as without it those that work in our hospitals cannot achieve more, which ultimately they will have to do. If you come to work with investment around you, productive, modern facilities working with you, life in any job can not only be pleasure but hugely productive as well. Sound facilities lead to happier patients. Happier patients feel more relaxed, communicate better, interact with the nursing staff and subsequently experience shorter recovery times. That means higher bed turnover and more targets achieved. And let's not forget how important food is. Let's make sure we invest both money and imagination into the catering facilities of our hospitals. Good food aids recovery!

We need to get to the point where the staff in every department of the hospital respect and enjoy the environment within which they work. It's not just about the environment however. The management in the hospital needs re analysing. Somewhere along the line PCT managers got hold of the hospitals at a cost to care standards. We all know what a difficult job this is. Managing limited resources, dealing with huge budgets, chasing funding and targets, coping with human resources, balancing the books, keeping everything going day to day, it's tough. I am sure that most of the people responsible for managing a hospital try their hardest to meet their objectives. Whether their objectives are right or not is a different conundrum. I wonder how many PCT's primary objective is to maximise patient care. Let's face it, PCT's seem to have spent large budgets on reorganisations but not on care facilities. A cursory glance at recent headlines from the latest financial performance report from the Department of Health would suggest that PCTs are responsible for 60 per cent of the gross national deficit (£793 million). Nearly half of PCTs are shown as being in deficit, compared to just over a third in 2005/6, so the position seems to be deteriorating. Whether these figures are accurate or not and it does depend on how they are interpreted since Health Authorities slice some funds off the PCT's figures for regional support, it is clear that not enough money is being made available to the PCTs and that the money in at least a third of the country's PCT s is not being managed efficiently or sustainably.

One of the worst days work in the management of hospitals was disbanding the concept of matrons. Everyone I talk to about the NHS from the patient side at least refers to the lack of basic supervision on the shop floor. The need to have someone whose sole responsibility is to maintain the standards of work at the very core of nursing seems such a sensible concept when ultimately these people are as responsible as any in the NHS to delivering patient care and recovery. At the same time the PCTs and the Government have to review the working practices of all of the staff in the hospitals. To have a situation whereby a nurse won't clean a dirty surface or act without a doctor present because of either litigious protocol or patient privacy is crazy. To have cleaners who are outside contractors and are not beholden to the hospital and not available 24, 7 is unacceptable. The whole concept of resource management and working practises needs reassessing. Time and motion studies need undertaking by people with a degree of imagination. The results will indicate that nurses spend almost a quarter of their time achieving no worthwhile function at all. That's not a criticism of nurses but one of the system and the role they have to perform. The problem for the NHS is that the entire system is as inefficient throughout the departments. An aside, I would like to see a few consultants told where to get off by a matron too. I know that ward managers exist today but having seen them in action they don't cut the mustard. Bring back matrons if you want to annihilate MRSA, square up overly confident consultants and produce an environment in which patients can have some confidence.

I would particularly like to see a real stickler in each and every A & E department. I actually agree with Tony Blair and his euphemism about A & E being the shop window of the NHS. Sadly A & E is not a pretty shop window. But it needs to be, and to achieve it they need the best people, the best resources, a high degree of support and continuing investment. To not have a sufficient admissions service bolted on to an A&E department in 2007 is a ludicrous situation, but one I experienced. The department is at the sharp end of saving lives and it needs brilliant people, from surgeons to cleaners, operating within it and they need modern sophisticated facilities.

Whatever does happen to the structures within the NHS it is obvious that without surgeons and consultants, the brains behind healthcare, we would be a lot worse off. Every day they deal with the human body and manage to perform what we consider to be miracles for our friends and family. Quite rightly they are revered and have some considerable standing within the organisation. We probably all have at least one of them to thank for our lives from our delivery in to this world and onward. However for many, how they deal with their patients is often under par and the number of people who have recounted desperate tales about their disappointing relationships with their specialists would fill a book. My experience in the NHS indicated that consultants can easily forget that they are dealing with people's lives. It must be very easy to see hundreds of different faces every week and begin to treat them as numbers. It must be a frustrating job at times dealing with the British public. It isn't difficult to imagine. However out of all of the people who take responsibility for how patients are treated they are in an exceptional position. Everyone around them takes a lead from their behaviour. I will never forget Con I standing at the end of my bed surrounded by his minions treating me as though I was an insignificant statistic in his round. He treated me with utter disdain and showed no respect for me as either a patient or a human being. I wonder what it taught all of his juniors huddled around him and dependent upon him for their first leg up. Consultants must not spend too much time in a huddle acting like God, sharing notes at technical meetings or sat in their consulting rooms listening to their own voices. They must keep in touch with the patients and be prepared to ask questions which might deliver difficult answers for them to listen to.

GP s, Government and the rest of the NHS have to re evaluate whether the golden contract has really benefited the system. I cannot see how paying people more to do less, works for anyone. I cannot believe any of us, as patients, are happy with the situation. But neither would we expect GPs to smash themselves to fragments working all of the hours god sends and for little reward. However somewhere in the middle there is a balance and the entire arrangement between the NHS and the GPs needs reassessing. Too much valuable cost which should be being directed to the benefit of the patient is finding its hands into individual's pockets and not being reinvested back in to the health service. I will probably make myself terribly unpopular with my own GP as a result of that statement. I hope not as I value his input greatly.

Finally the organisation needs teamwork at every level. A combination of brave leadership, sound management, staff with the work ethic and human values to boot, just like my angels will improve the present situation. We need people with a belief in the NHS vision, sound structures, good staffing levels and facilities for staff and patients alike to enable everyone's motivations to be met. Whilst IT is important and lends itself to faster and larger levels of communication, only good human communication skills will enable all of the teams, large and small and in whatever department to achieve their goals. Everyone has to come to work wanting to make people well again and wanting the organisation to succeed.

As I have mentioned before and for fear of repeating myself, I am no expert. Yet all of the points I have made seem common sense, I hope, and I wonder why they are missed by those with the authority to manage the changes required. If everyone realised what went on behind closed doors, if politicians took the time to really enter the NHS and find out what it was really like to be hospitalised, if all of the patients complained about the conditions, if the staff pushed harder for improvements in their facilities, if we all opened our eyes to what went on and if we all learnt to shout a little bit louder I wonder what we could achieve. Maybe you will write to your MP; at least it's a start. Now could be a good time to be heard as Gordon Brown has already made promises about reviewing the NHS.

Someone recently asked me, what was the one thing which I had learnt from my experience? What stuck with me the most? Just before I was asked the question, I had been listening to a Jeremy Vine debate on Radio 2 about various issues within the NHS. Vine had said something to which I agreed in principle but then I also had great sympathy with the caller whose point Vine disagreed. It stood out for obvious reasons. Jeremy Vine had read an email sent in by a previous patient under the NHS who had experienced concerning degrees of unhygienic activity on a ward. A nurse had dropped a canula on the floor, picked it up and continued to try and insert it into the patient's arm. The patient had gone potty and shouted at the nurse. Jeremy had suggested it was rather unnecessary to shout at nurses. 'They are doing their best'. I sort of understood where he was coming from but couldn't help but feel that in the same position he might have done exactly the same thing. As I remembered the point and considered the question before me it was clear that the 'one thing' was to shout when you needed to. To shout with all of the might you have in your lungs because in fact it might be the one thing that kept you alive. I know it must be disconcerting for a nurse to have some 'Mr Angry' in front of you but unless we are prepared to complain, state our case, recognise substandard activity and protect our own self interest and care about our own well being, we will neither get well nor improve the system. No one else shouts for you in the NHS, you have to learn to do it for yourself. I know it sounds melodramatic but literally shouting the loudest can save your life.

Parties.

On a perfect summer's evening, which in a flooded 2007 was a miracle in itself, I managed to have the party I promised myself as I lay on my A & E trolley. 80 people arrived to find barrels of beer, a hog roast, an evening of beautiful English weather as well as a disco which kept half the village up until the early hours. Many guests were forced into taxis at the end of the evening as they just didn't want to really go home. It will be remembered for a long time as a great party.

Despite being the host and having responsibilities I found a few quieter moments. I stood back from the fray and looked in to a scene of such fun and happiness. It seemed a universe away from the almost surreal experience I had suffered at the hands of the NHS earlier in the year. I realised firstly how very lucky I had been and also what a wonderful thing life is despite the adversity we sometimes all face. It seemed to me that at times in order to value the life you lead you need to face adversity and even have your life hung in a balance to fully realise how fortunate we are to have its gift. The perspective one enjoys when coming through a significant experience is certainly a very valuable event.

In one year I had undergone a transformation. I had changed my career, my personal life and through it all my health had been a significant issue. I had found myself with a new job, a new relationship and lots of opportunities; although not necessarily in the direction I had initially chosen. On top of that all of the important people in my life were around me and I have been reminded on a number of occasions that I have certainly been blessed with good friends.

When I lay on the trolley in A&E I had no idea as the direction my life would take and whether my health would allow me a normal life. It felt like my life was in a tumble drier on spin. I could see the outside world through the door glass, but I just couldn't stop the cycle so that I could open the drier door and get out. I have been extremely lucky and I am eternally grateful. I am now able to lead an almost normal life. It seems ridiculous that it has taken the best part of twenty years to resolve my condition.

Food is no longer a devil and I can eat almost anything within reason. My strategy of keeping fit, eating sensibly, maintaining a balanced diet and taking probiotics seems to be working for me. If I hadn't been so forceful or so interested in my own self preservation I wonder what a greater reliance upon a consultant's advice would have left me. I wonder what may have happened to me had I not shouted.

I continue to have a clouded view of the medical profession and a mistrust of some of the services the NHS offers us. I have been very lucky. Others are not and I believe it could have gone far worse for me and as a result I might never have been able to enjoy my party. I think often about the carnage my life would have suffered from as a result of surgery for instance. I often remember the difficulties that some of the people I met on my way suffer from. And it is with them in mind that I end by wishing all of the people I met in hospital a speedy recovery and a long and happy life too. I would also like to thank those who cared for me, or at least those who deserve thanks.

Finally I wish all of you, who have shown an interest and hopefully enjoyed my tale, all health and happiness – wealth too. But since you can't have all three things allegedly and I know which two are priceless, I'm settling for the first two.

I only wish those who are running the NHS would do the same as they analyse their priorities for patient care.

About the Author

Born and bred in North Lincolnshire, Ed Davey has been a leading figure in the local farming community for twenty years. Educated at Harper Adams he returned home to help run the family farming business in 1986 and remained there until 2006. After various life changing experiences he set up as the National Farmer's Union Group Secretary for the Holderness region in East Yorkshire in July 2007. He is passionate about the farming industry and the countryside he lives and works in. One of the hardest working farmers in the region he would be usually found out on the farm every hour god sent applying himself to the perpetual battle against nature to produce vegetables and combineable crops on the 550 ha farm Throughout the last five years he has worked particulalrly hard, often without a day off in a year and working extremely long hours week in week out to achieve his goals. In his few hours of free time he has written various articles for the farming press and figured in the Farmer's Weekly Awards in 2006 where he was runner up in the Arable Farmer of the year category. 'He who shouts loudest' is his first book. Ed has been considering writing a novel for some time but it was his experience during a recent illness which inspired his literary desires and once pen went to paper he was always going to create his first piece about his extraordinary journey through the NHS. Ed lives still in North Lincolnshire and whilst still involved in the family farming business focuses most of his energy over the River Humber supporting the farmers of Holderness.